Alston Moor, Cumbria

Buildings in a North Pennines landscape

T0340610

Alston Moor, Cumbria

Buildings in a North Pennines landscape

Lucy Jessop and Matthew Whitfield, with Andrew Davison

ENGLISH HERITAGE

Published by English Heritage, The Engine House, Fire Fly Avenue, Swindon SN2 2EH
www.english-heritage.org.uk
English Heritage is the Government's statutory adviser on all aspects of the historic environment.

© English Heritage 2013

Images (except as otherwise shown) © English Heritage or © Crown copyright. EH.

First published 2013

ISBN 978-1-84802-117-4
Product code 51755

British Library Cataloguing in Publication Data
A CIP catalogue record for this book is available from the British Library.

All rights reserved
No part of this publication may be reproduced or transmitted in any form or by any means, electronic or mechanical, including photocopying, recording, or any information storage or retrieval system, without permission in writing from the publisher.

Application for the reproduction of images should be made to English Heritage. Every effort has been made to trace the copyright holders and we apologise in advance for any unintentional omissions, which we would be pleased to correct in any subsequent edition of this book.

For more information about images from the English Heritage Archive, contact Archive Services Team, The Engine House, Fire Fly Avenue, Swindon SN2 2EH; telephone (01793) 414600.

Brought to publication by Sarah Enticknap, Publishing, English Heritage
Edited by Wendy Toole
Page layout by Pauline Hull
Principal photography by Alun Bull, English Heritage
Printed in the UK by Butler Tanner & Dennis Ltd

Front cover
High Lovelady Shield, a ruined vernacular farmhouse in Alston Moor.
[DP154200]

Inside front cover
Terrain map of Alston Moor.

Opposite title page
An Alston Moor farmhouse in its North Pennines setting.
[DP154255]

Contents

Foreword

Alston Moor is a very special place. Its wild, upland environment is beautiful; its vernacular buildings are unusual and individual. Human endeavour has shaped this landscape, leaving tantalising traces for us to discover. The historic environment of this isolated corner of Cumbria encapsulates two major strands: farming and mining. Agriculture, Alston Moor's first and most enduring industry, supported its earliest settlements; today many farmsteads carry on the tradition of hill farming that has sustained the area for millennia and that contributed to the development and prosperity of the market town of Alston. The area's mineral wealth, exploited since Roman times, had brought a rising population to the parish by the end of the 18th century. The rakes, spoil heaps and buildings of the mining industry remain as monuments to one of Alston Moor's most exciting periods, when the price of lead dictated the direction of a man's life.

Change is always part of an area's story: buildings and landscapes have always responded to economic ups and downs, the rise and fall of industries and fluctuations in population. The last two centuries brought many challenges to Alston Moor but, remarkably, much of the rich legacy of its history has survived, particularly in the form of its vernacular buildings and its workers' villages, all set against the backdrop of the spectacular surrounding fells. Opportunities exist here to revitalise and breathe new life into a variety of historic buildings, making them fit for purpose while treating them sensitively and appropriately.

This is the first book in English Heritage's Informed Conservation series to consider a complete parish and to look at buildings within their archaeological context and rural landscape.

Dr Simon Thurley
Chief Executive, English Heritage

Acknowledgements

Many colleagues at English Heritage contributed to this book. Research and survey work in Alston Moor was principally carried out by Lucy Jessop and Matthew Whitfield, with Adam Menuge, Simon Taylor, Garry Corbett, Allan T Adams, Rachel M Cross and Nigel Fradgley. Research support was provided by Laura Holland and Kate Bould. The authors would like to thank Adam Menuge for his editorial role and insightful comments and Colum Giles for his helpful clarifications. We are very grateful to Dave Went, Al Oswald, Stewart Ainsworth and Jeremy Lake who kindly contributed to some of the text concerned with the wider landscape, archaeology of the area and the character of farmsteads, as well as commenting upon the whole. Dave MacLeod, Matthew Oakey and Sally Evans provided much useful information on the archaeology of the area as seen from above, as well as producing aerial photographs and lidar images commissioned by English Heritage from Infoterra. We would also like to thank our illustrator Allan T Adams and our principal photographer Alun Bull, without whose work this book would have been so much poorer. Other photographs were taken by the authors, Bob Skingle and Naomi Archer, with additional images provided by the English Heritage Archive; the maps were drawn by Philip Sinton. The book was brought to publication by Sarah Enticknap of English Heritage Publishing.

The authors would like to thank the staff of Cumbria Archives Service, Carlisle (CAS); the National Archives, London (TNA); the North of England Institute of Mining and Mechanical Engineers, Newcastle (NEIMME); and Durham University Library (DUL) for their help on this project. We are very grateful for permission from the Cumbria Archives Service, Carlisle Library, the North of England Institute of Mining and Mechanical Engineers, the English Heritage Archive, the National Archives and the Science Museum for allowing us to reproduce images from documents held in their collections.

This book would not have been possible without the kindness of Alastair Robertson, who introduced us to the Alston Moor Historical Society and to many people and buildings that we would not otherwise have encountered; he also commented on the text of this book. Finally, we wish to thank the people of Alston Moor, and particularly all the owners and occupiers of the buildings that we investigated, for their warmth and friendliness throughout our work in the parish.

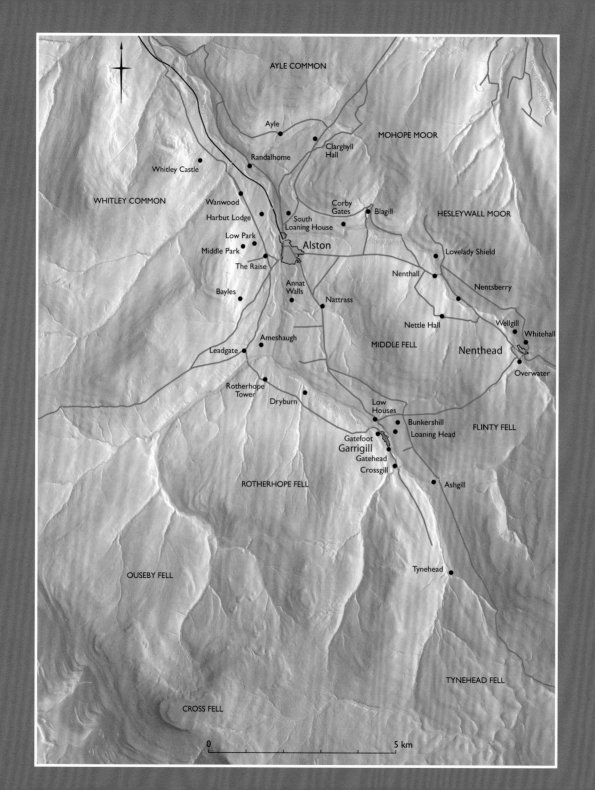

AYLE COMMON

MOHOPE MOOR

Ayle

Clarghyll
Hall

Randalhome

Whitley Castle

WHITLEY COMMON

Wanwood

Corby
Gates

Blagill

HESLEYWALL MOOR

Harbut Lodge

South
Loaning House

Low Park

Alston

Lovelady Shield

Middle Park

Nenthall

Nentsberry

The Raise

Bayles

Annat
Walls

Nattrass

Nettle Hall

Wellgill

Whitehall

MIDDLE FELL

Nenthead

Ameshaugh

Leadgate

Overwater

Rotherhope
Tower

Dryburn

Low
Houses

Bunkershill

Loaning Head

FLINTY FELL

Gatefoot

Garrigill

Gatehead

Crossgill

Ashgill

ROTHERHOPE FELL

OUSEBY FELL

Tynehead

TYNEHEAD FELL

CROSS FELL

0   5 km

1

Introduction

Alston Moor sits on the eastern edge of Cumbria, in historic Cumberland, creating a border for the county with Northumberland and County Durham (Fig 1). But proximity to another border – that with Scotland, just 13 miles (21km) to the north – has shaped its evolution much more powerfully. It is a place of high fells, wreathed in clouds and mists, swept by the wind and the rain. In fine weather it is transformed into a place of dramatic skies, with rich and varied colours and textures. Higher areas have a covering of rough grass and heather, which contrasts with the richer green pasture of the lower valley sides and bottoms; the two are connected by numerous streams and waterfalls. This landscape is home to much of England's population of black grouse and teems with biodiversity. For human habitation there is the small market town of Alston, scattered farmsteads and a handful of villages and hamlets, some perched on the steep-sided valleys of the South Tyne and Nent rivers and others making use of the valley bottoms (Fig 2). Alston Moor is a place which man has exploited for millennia, through industry and agriculture, to gain a scanty livelihood or to make a fortune.

The fells encircle the two river valleys, Alston, the villages of Nenthead and Garrigill and the dispersed settlements that help to define the character of the area. At 2,930 feet (893 metres) above sea level, Cross Fell, on the southwest fringe of the parish, is the highest point in the Pennines; the water collected there and on Tynehead Fell feeds into the South Tyne. Middle Fell occupies the centre of the area between the Nent and South Tyne valleys; at 1,886 feet (575 metres), it was home to some of the richest lead seams in the area. Smaller fells and commons lie to the north and south, all in the region of 1,640–2,000 feet (500–600 metres) in height. With its market place situated at 967 feet (295 metres) above sea level, Alston has a strong claim to be England's highest market town, a title also claimed by Buxton, in Derbyshire.

The English Heritage project

In 2008, English Heritage commenced a wide-ranging interdisciplinary investigation to examine the miner-farmer landscapes of the North Pennines Area of Outstanding Natural Beauty (AONB). This project, dedicated to exploring the history of the area through its archaeological and architectural remains, was

Figure 1
The parish of Alston Moor, with its principal settlements.

devised in response to emerging threats from climate change and new social and economic trends. Alston Moor, as the parish at the heart of the AONB, was selected as the main area of study: it possessed the principal market town of the area and had been a major centre of mineral extraction, which for many centuries, alongside agriculture, had been the principal industry of the North Pennines. This book presents only a small part of English Heritage's research carried out in the course of the project; it concentrates on examining the development of the surviving buildings in Alston Moor from the earliest vernacular structures to those of the present day. It considers the contribution of those buildings to the special character of the parish's wider landscape and explores the ways in which their future can be assured to the benefit both of that landscape and of the community as a whole.

Figure 2
The hamlet of Dryburn, situated above the South Tyne valley, surrounded by dispersed settlement and mining remains.
[DP154141]

An upland environment

Agriculture has historically been the dominant industry in the area and is still a major part of its economy today; it exploits Alston Moor's large expanses of high, poorly drained ground by using it largely for pastoral farming. As in most other upland landscapes, the difficult terrain has limited the locations suitable for permanent settlement and virtually dictated the course of transport routes. The harsh climate has forced most people to avoid exposed positions, and the scanty income derived from upland agriculture led people to build solid, utilitarian, unornamented dwellings. A cool, damp climate and a short growing season have made arable farming generally less feasible than in the lowlands, while rocky outcrops, steep slopes, bogs, and thin or heavy soils have further reduced the area available for ploughing. This in turn has restricted the options for settlement location and building materials. For example, straw thatch, a by-product of cereal cultivation, would appear to have been little used since prehistoric times, when houses were fewer and smaller; and as most of the area's woodland seems to have been cleared at an early date, the extensive use of timber framing was simply out of the question by the medieval period. Stone, however, was in plentiful supply, heather grew on the deforested moors and, as we shall see, buildings could be simply constructed then roofed using heather thatch. Yet if the uplands imposed many restrictions, they also offered many opportunities which led humans to defy their oppressive environment, sometimes with extraordinary audacity. The same circumstances that restricted arable farming conversely gave rise to a finely tuned system of land and livestock management, which was accompanied by particular building types and settlement patterns.

Mineral extraction

The mineral veins that criss-cross the complex North Pennines ore field have long been exploited, from the Roman period onwards, providing a second strand for the local economy. Lead, and the silver that could be derived from it, are undoubtedly the region's best-known natural treasures. The high rainfall which limits agriculture (and is now bemoaned by tourists and residents alike)

Figure 3
Miners walking to work, depicted in a volume of drawings
of lead mining in the North Pennines, dated between
1800 and 1820.
[© Science Museum/Science & Society Picture Library]

fed the streams which supplied water power for milling corn, crushing and washing ore, ventilating mines and many other tasks, and created the peat bogs that provided abundant fuel for both industrial and domestic use. Lead was just one of a wide spectrum of geological resources that could be profitably exploited, including – importantly for this study – a range of readily available building materials: limestone for mortar and sandstone for walls, roofs and carved mouldings. As a result, the story of human achievement on Alston Moor has never been one of mere passive adaptation to a tyrannical environment, but one of clever, ambitious and at times highly imaginative exploitation of the resources that exist here in a unique combination (Fig 3). Indeed, so successful has this past human endeavour been that we may question whether 'Area of Outstanding *Artificial* Beauty' would be a more appropriate term for this highly valued and protected landscape.

It has long been assumed, undoubtedly correctly, that the great Roman outpost fort known since at least the 17th century as Whitley Castle (in Latin probably *Epiacum*) was sited to oversee the extraction, collection and transhipment of silver-rich lead (also known as galena). Although the sites where the ore was smelted remain to be found, the resulting ingots were probably taken north to Hadrian's Wall via a military road known as the Maiden Way, long stretches of which remain visible across Alston Moor. It is also possible, though less probable, that the ingots were taken south over the high ground to the Stainmore forts. Yet until recently almost no evidence had been recognised for the network of extraction sites, nor for the communities of local miners who must have fed the galena back to Whitley Castle, sitting like a spider at the heart of this web (Fig 4).

Figure 4
Aerial photograph of Whitley Castle.
[20677/049]

The population of the parish is intrinsically linked to the success, and failure, of the mineral extraction industry; the number of people living in Alston Moor today is barely double the estimate of 555 from 1687–8.[1] As the lead seams were increasingly exploited throughout the 18th century, the population of the parish rapidly increased, reaching a peak of 6,858 people in 1831. The massive instability in lead prices for the next 30 years resulted in a fluctuating, then falling, number of inhabitants: by 1891, Alston Moor was home to 3,384 people.[2] But once the industry completely withdrew from the parish, the speed of desertion increased even further; by 2001 the population had fallen to 1,128, a third of the 1891 level. The buildings of Alston Moor were at different times adapted and extended, or abandoned and demolished, in response to population change, shaping the landscape of the town, villages and dispersed settlements that we see today.

Tourism

Of the two industries that had such an indelible effect on the landscape of Alston Moor, agriculture and mineral extraction, only agriculture endures today – now, in the 21st century, this is mostly dependent on sheep farming. Manufacturing has continued as a small-scale presence in the parish's economy, and many businesses and creative industries thrive, but today it is often the visitor and tourist that Alston Moor serves. Unlike the Lake District, the North Pennines had to wait until the later 20th century to be discovered by mass tourism, although the grouse moors were already being exploited by the end of the 19th century for those better-off visitors whose inclination ran to shooting game. Even those who knew and loved the area realised that its harsh landscape and environment could be both appealing and repellent to visitors, depending upon the weather (Fig 5). Thomas Sopwith, a mine agent and sometime Alstonian, wrote in 1833 about the place where he had lived and worked for four years in his youth:

The houses scattered over the lower parts of the hills are nearly all whitewashed, and thus impart some liveliness to a scene in which wildness and sterility much prevail. It has been justly observed that the appearance

Figure 5
Houses in upper Teesdale, County Durham – here, just to the south of Alston Moor, the tradition of painted walls survives. Whitewashed buildings were once common in Alston Moor.
[DP154183]

of these districts is peculiarly affected by different kinds of weather. On a
fine sunny day most strangers are pleased and highly interested by the
prospects throughout this part of the vale of the South Tyne, while, on the
contrary, a rainy day … presents a spectacle of extreme dreariness, which
has contributed to the erroneous but very prevailing idea of Alston Moor
being a treeless, miserable waste.[3]

Today, by bicycle, on foot, or by car, people come to the area to admire the
majesty of the moorland scenery, walk the fells, explore the historic town of
Alston and visit the remains of its industrial heritage.

Settlement and building patterns

As the following chapters will show, the landscape and buildings of Alston Moor
give clues to the nature of post-medieval life quite readily, but the evidence for
earlier patterns of settlement and land use is harder to identify: most traces
survive only as low earthworks in the fields and on the moors. Roman and pre-
Roman land use has, until recently, been something of an enigma. Fortunately,
although proof of Roman mines themselves remains elusive, English Heritage's
campaign of research has now identified dozens of small settlements, all remarkably well preserved as earthworks owing to the scarcity of medieval and later
ploughing, and each containing a handful of small roundhouses where some of
the native miners must have lived. Many of these settlements are likely to have
had their origins in the Iron Age (c 700 BC–AD 70) or even the later Bronze Age
(after about 1000 BC).

There is a clear pattern in their choice of location in relation to the river valleys, a pattern so strong that it seems a safe bet that the medieval town of Alston
was built on top of one. The largest of the native settlements is a village
of at least 14 separate family groups, organised on either side of a trackway
immediately north of Alston at Gossipgate, and set within ancient field boundaries whose presence may be reflected in the name of a nearby 18th-century farm,
'Banks' (Fig 6). Here and elsewhere long stretches of the dry stone walls that
define the upper limit of the improved pastures of later centuries are now known
to follow earlier earthen 'head dykes' constructed in the late Iron Age or earlier.

Figure 6
*Lidar image of the late Iron Age or Romano-British
village above Gossipgate. The village was approached
by a hollow way (bottom left) and sits within a
contemporary lyncheted field system; later medieval
and post-medieval ploughing are also visible. The
present Gossipgate Farm and the river Nent are at the
bottom of the image.*

These great earthworks, some running for miles along the valley sides, each had a ditch above the bank to carry water away from the slopes below. Without these simple yet impressive engineering works, the conditions that permitted prehistoric and medieval arable agriculture, and eventually the lush species-rich meadows we see today, might never have existed.

As the mining industry expanded and the population of Alston Moor climbed, the scatter of isolated farmsteads that now typifies the region settled into its current state. Although seemingly random, the positions of these remote farmsteads are, in fact, rooted in a layout of fields and tracks that has developed through preceding centuries if not millennia. These positions are clearly defined, lying between the valley bottoms and the spring line on the edge of the moors. In short, the post-medieval buildings and fields we see today hang like a thin veil across a landscape with a much more ancient heritage.

The special nature of Alston Moor's built environment

This heritage, encompassing a heavily worked agricultural and industrial land-scape, the natural beauties of the high fells and sheltered valleys and an impressive array of vernacular buildings, has baffled, interested and impressed both inhabitants and visitors for centuries. The buildings, as we will see, were often described as poor and old-fashioned, but their unusual design, on which much of this book will concentrate, went disregarded. It was not until 1811 that the special nature of the buildings of eastern Cumberland was first men-tioned, in Jollie's *Cumberland Guide & Directory*:

> About the north and east confines of the county, a few houses of a singular construction yet remain; the walls of which are very thick and strong, and besides the little well-secured windows, often contain a sort of port-holes. The cattle and their owners resided under the same roof; the former occupied the ground floor, and the latter the upper storey.[4]

These observations were not, of course, limited to the buildings of Alston Moor, but they made the first attempt at describing the area's most characteris-tic farmstead type, with agricultural usage of the ground floor combined with domestic accommodation above. This is the bastle, which will be discussed throughout this book (Fig 7). Several features mark out the area as a place of particular interest: bastles and the vernacular buildings, both rural and urban, derived from them are perhaps the most special of Alston Moor's building types, but the parish's historic environment is also enhanced by the develop-

Figure 7
Annat Walls, c 1900, a farmstead constructed from a
row of many bastle-like elements.
[© Carlisle Library, Cumbria County Council]

ment of Nenthead from a tiny hamlet into a centre of lead mining in the early 19th century.

Alston Moor's buildings reflect many of the strands of life as experienced by this disparate upland community over time: the struggle to live and work in a harsh natural environment, the reaction to long periods of insecurity and instability, and the endeavour to adapt to the rise and fall of industries. Houses, farmsteads, places of worship and places of work all evolved to meet the needs of the people who lived, worshipped and worked within them. Various building types reflect a response to the challenges of life in the parish and were developed accordingly, sometimes in rather special ways. This book celebrates the endeavours of Alston Moor's residents in the face of the harshness of their natural environment by telling the story of their buildings.

2
Agrarian Alston Moor, 1130–1770

Alston Moor in the Middle Ages was a wild and isolated place, dominated by the high, heather-clad fells. When the antiquarian William Camden visited Cumberland, Carlisle and Hadrian's Wall in the late 16th century, he described the county's eastern part thus: 'pars Orientalior macra licet illa, ieiuna, & solitaria'; translated into English, 'its Eastern part is lean, hungry, and a waste'.[5] Trees were few and were concentrated in the valleys, shadowed by the brooding, peaty backdrop of Cross Fell, Flinty Fell and Black Fell. However, deep within those fells lay sources of immense wealth – vast deposits of silver-rich lead – and in the sheltered South Tyne and Nent valleys livestock could be raised and fattened and some crops grown (Fig 8). The continuity of settlement from pre-history to the present day demonstrates that the difficulties of living, working and travelling in such an inclement upland environment were eminently surmountable and that the landscape, however harsh, was exploitable.

The medieval manor of Alston Moor

The documented history of the manor of Alston Moor commences in the early 12th century, when Henry I's Pipe Roll for 1130–1 refers to Carlisle's silver mine, later shown to be in Alston Moor. At this date, Alston Moor was owned by the king of Scotland, for which feudal rights he did homage to the king of England who retained the all-important rights of mineral exploitation beneath the ground.[6] Around 1209, William the Lion of Scotland granted the estate to William de Veteripont and it remained in the possession of the Veteripont family even after 1296, when the manor became the property of the English crown after it forcibly appropriated the English estates of the Scottish king, John Baliol.[7] The Veteripontes appear to have been of Norman origin, their name a Latinisation of the old French 'vieux pont' meaning 'old bridge', so named after the village of Vieux-Pont-en-Auge, Calvados. Variations and contractions of this surname survive in the parish to this day, including Vipond and Vipont.

In the early 15th century, the Stapleton family inherited the lordship of the manor following the marriage of Walter Stapleton (d 1457) to a Veteripont daughter; one of the daughters of this marriage married Sir William Hilton, bringing the manor to the Hilton family. These families do not appear to have had a major seat in Alston Moor, although the presence of the Old Manor at

Figure 8
Cross Fell and the head of the South Tyne valley.
[DP154354]

Lowbyer suggests that manorial functions – such as the collection of rents and the dispensing of justice – were once carried out there. Their centres of power lay elsewhere in northern England and Scotland: branches of the Veteriponte family owned land around Linlithgow in Scotland, as well as Brougham Castle near Penrith, and Bowes; the Hiltons' principal seat was Hilton (or Hylton) Castle near Sunderland, now in the guardianship of English Heritage. Priorsdale, an area between Nenthead and Cross Fell, has a manorial history separate from the rest of the modern parish; as its name suggests, it was held by Hexham Priory until the latter's dissolution in 1537.

A picture of the Veteripontes' manor of Alston Moor is found in an inquest on the death of Nicholas de Veteriponte in 1315.[8] The principal settlements of Alston, Garrigill and the Nent valley were clearly well established by this date. The document also mentions other substantial settlements in the vicinity of Ameshaugh and Corby Gates – Ameshaugh sits on the sheltered, low-lying land of the South Tyne valley while Corby Gates (meaning 'crow roads') lies on the north side of the Nent valley, to the west of Blagill. Veteriponte's capital messuage was accompanied by 14 acres of arable land and 100 acres of meadow. The manor had 33 tenants in Garrigill who had 23 shielings, and 13 tenants at Ameshaugh; the 22 tenants at Nent and Corby Gates had 22 shielings. Shielings indicate the practice of transhumance – the seasonal movement of livestock to summer pastures, which in upland country are typically on the higher ground. The lack of shielings associated with Ameshaugh suggests that this lower settlement did not have distinct summer pastures associated with it. The manor also owned a water corn mill and a fulling mill, and held 3,000 acres of pasture. In the estimation of William Wallace, an early historian of the area, this number of tenants suggested that the manor of Alston Moor contained a community of between 500 and 600 people.[9] Until the reorganisation of the manor in the early 17th century, tenants held their properties from the manor by copyhold.

The 14 acres of arable land mentioned in the inquisition formed an extremely small proportion of the manor's land; the majority of its land consisted of vast expanses of pasture on the fells, providing grazing for both cattle and sheep, while the meadow ground supplied the hay crop necessary for the over-wintering of the beasts. Some of the lower valley hillsides around Banks, Rotherhope and Ayle show signs of arable cultivation, their lynchets probably dating from the 13th and 14th centuries. Ashgill, Bayles, Blagill, Bleagate, Crossgill, Dryburn, Gossipgate, Nentsberry, Priorsdale and Wanwood are further examples of place names recorded during this period, but with varied spelling; some appeared in documents as far back as the first half of the 13th century.

Following recent archaeological investigations, it is now considered possible that Nicholas de Veteriponte's 'capital messuage' or principal dwelling was in Alston, at Hall Hill, to the west of Alston on the western side of the South Tyne river. The origins of this intriguing earthwork have long been in doubt, but it is now recognised as a diminutive and basic ringwork castle, similar to Kirby Lonsdale on the River Lune, carved out of a prominent natural ridge (Fig 9). Ringwork castles were largely constructed during the 12th century;

Figure 9
Two sides of the ringwork castle are clearly shown by the lidar image, cut into a natural moraine mound. The castle sits on the west bank of the South Tyne, across the river from Alston.

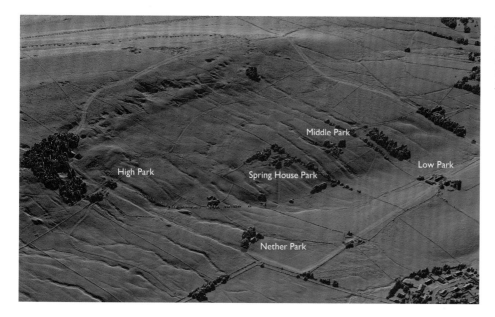

Middle Park

Low Park

High Park

Spring House Park

Nether Park

Figure 10
Lidar image looking north-westwards of
the former hunting park to the west of
Alston, showing its boundary (highlighted)
and the profusion of park-related names
for its farmsteads.

this one may date to the early time of Veteriponte involvement in the area. The ridge commanded what would have been an important river crossing, immediately upstream from the confluence of the South Tyne and the Nent, and would have been the forerunner to a succession of bridges located yet further upstream.

The Veteripontes continued to improve their manor by creating a hunting park within easy reach of their seat in Alston: in 1337, Robert de Veteriponte was granted permission to empark his wood at Wanwood, to the west of Alston. This suggests that an area in the vicinity of the castle was enclosed and bounded by a park pale: a palisade or wall set upon a bank with a ditch on the inner side to prevent the lord's deer from escaping (Fig 10). The ringwork itself, which shows no indication of significant military improvement, may have been transformed into a comfortable hunting lodge for the occasional use of the lord and his guests. The park is now represented by some curving field boundaries and a scatter of park-related place names on the west side of the Tyne, with the farms of Nether Park, High Park, Middle Park and Low Park all sitting on the eastern slopes of Park Fell.

Many of de Veteriponte's tenants lived in the vicinity of Garrigill, spelled Gerardgill in the 1315 inquisition, a village which was formed from a loose association of farmsteads situated around the junction of several trackways used both for driving livestock up onto the fells and for the transportation of minerals from the mines. Garrigill was large enough, and distant enough from the parish church of St Augustine in Alston, to receive a chapel to minister to the needs of the village and its outlying settlements by 1215.

Wallace mentions earthen banks and ditches set up 'at some remote period' along the valley sides to separate the high summer grazing land from the enclosed fields which yielded the vital hay crop for winter fodder, forming 'the outside boundaries of the ancient tenements or shieldings [sic]'.[10] Extensive lengths of these head dykes still survive, with notable examples found along the north side of the Nent Valley between High Spencycroft and Corby Gates, on the north side of the South Tyne from Low Sillyhall to Cropshall, and across Fairhill on the east side of the Tyne south of Alston (Fig 11). Wallace says that these dykes appear to have formed the boundaries of the 'ancient tenements or

Figure 11
Lidar image looking eastwards along the head dyke at Corby Gates.

shielings' mentioned in the Alston 'Paine Roll' of 1597, and in this he is certainly correct. Furthermore, recent fieldwork has also shown that Wallace's astute suggestion that the boundaries originated far earlier – 'at a considerable period before the Conquest' – is also true. Typically these dykes enclose field systems of smaller banks and ditches, or narrow terraces (lynchets) formed by ancient cultivation, radiating from small clusters of late Iron Age or Romano-British hut circles. Above Gossipgate, in the Nent valley, the head dyke is overlain by the remains of two such settlements, proving that it is older still and perhaps Bronze Age in origin. The remarkable fact is that, once established, these ancient boundaries retained their significance over the ensuing centuries. They provide the framework for medieval charters such as a grant of land in the valley south of Alston recorded in the Black Book of Hexham Priory in 1232, as well as for the sort of customary rights and responsibilities mentioned in the Paine Roll. As such, they remained an important element in the farming land-scape right up to the enclosure of the moors and wastes in the 19th century.

The manor's dependence on animal husbandry was clear, with the average of one tenant per shieling in this period in the Nent Valley and slightly more than one tenant per shieling elsewhere. The shieling (also 'shiel' or 'shield') is usually defined as a small cottage or hut, usually dry stone walled, windowless and roofed with turf, where a herdsman could shelter close to his sheep and cattle once they were brought up to graze on the high pastures during the summer months. Curiously, in this case no trace of any buildings has been rec-ognised, although other, possibly later examples, such as those in Gilderdale near Whitley Castle, have left very distinct remains. The existence of shielings is perpetuated in place names across the parish, such as Lovelady Shield, Shieldhill and Shield Hilltop. The Alston Moor Paine Roll, compiled in 1597 but based on a document from the reign of Henry VII (1485–1509), states that ten-ants should go to the 'sheles' within a month from St Helen's day (3 May) and return by St Peter's day (1 August).[11] This is a considerably shorter grazing period than in other landscapes, including the Yorkshire Dales, where it would be usual to leave the cattle out from the start of May until well into October.

Although the cattle would have had a higher value per head, sheep were also valuable, both for their wool and for their meat. The presence of a fulling mill in the parish is evidence that the inhabitants were engaged in producing cloth from local wool; once the sheep were shorn, the wool was spun and woven into cloth, then finished by being fulled (or felted) by water-powered hammers in the manor's mill. The tracks on which the animals were driven from the farmsteads up to the high pastures and shielings on the fells were called loanings; today, two hamlets bear that name, one to the north of Alston and the other to the north-east of Garrigill.

The early development of the town of Alston

The earliest documented form of Alston's name is *Altounby*, *-by* denoting a farmstead in Norse, the language prevalent across much of the North for almost two centuries before 1066. The Norse word gives us the modern term 'byre', meaning a cattle shed, and Lowbyer, once the seat of Alston's manorial local government, may be the site of another Norse farmstead. Later, Alston's name varies between Aldreston, Aldstone and Alston, with Auster-More frequently used as the name of the parish. The name Gossipgate, now applied both to a lane in Alston and to a former hamlet higher up the Nent valley, was first documented in the 14th century, but the 'gate' element derives from another Norse word: *yat*, meaning a street or way (in this case the track that connected Alston with the former hamlet and places beyond). Many small, circular, prehistoric settlements have been found in the course of the English Heritage project, positioned on similar contours above the river valleys. The circular shape of Alston's churchyard suggests that the settlement of Alston originated from one of these, with the church later positioned within the circular enclosure (Fig 12).

Alston's position, at the confluence of the rivers Nent and South Tyne and at the junction of several early routes, ensured its emergence as the most significant settlement in the parish. As the settlement expanded, buildings were erected along the principal trackways and formed a small network of roads: The Butts led towards Gossipgate, and Townfoot linked the town to Lowbyer and Garrigill via crossings of the two rivers, while Townhead provided access to the settlements of the Nent valley. Front Street, the principal thoroughfare, flanked the churchyard and joined all of these roads together; its central point became the natural situation for the market place. A stream ran from the highest area of the town at Fair Hill, skirting the eastern fringes of Front Street,

Figure 12 (opposite page)
Aerial photograph of Alston, showing the curved
enclosure around the churchyard.
[20682/022]

through The Butts and down to the Nent. This burn would increasingly provide water power and sluicing for the town's industrial processing, eventually supporting a forge and two corn mills by the mid-18th century. The vertiginous situation of Alston, clinging to the hillside with a climb of 30 metres up the length of Front Street from Townhead to Townfoot, did not prevent its rise to local pre-eminence (Fig 13). Indeed, Alston was positioned above the flood-prone river valleys, and most settlements in the immediate area would have had to deal with a similarly challenging gradient.

Although no definitive information is available to confirm the foundation of a parish church in Alston, it appears that one was established by 1154, when Henry II appointed Galfrid as rector of St Augustine's. It can probably be

Figure 13 (right)
Front Street, Alston, above the market place,
looking towards the south-east, photographed by
John Gay c 1950.
[AA081229]

assumed that Alston's dominant position, serving the surrounding scattered mining and farming communities, had been established by this date. Alston's medieval church survived until 1769, when it was demolished and rebuilt. It contained a shrine or chapel dedicated to Our Lady – a will of 1585 refers to the 'ladye porche' within which the testator wished to be buried.[12] The ecclesiastical parish of Alston fell within the diocese of Durham, and in 1338 the prior of Hexham was given the revenues of the parish by the Bishop of Durham, something that a previous prior had petitioned for in 1334 to fund his restoration of Hexham Priory after it had been partially destroyed by Scottish raiders. The parish was reassigned to the newly created bishopric of Newcastle in 1882.

Life and work in Alston Moor

Farming was central to the lives of the people of Alston Moor, supplying sustenance and some income to the majority of families in the area. The manor's lands were divided into tenements, named after the principal farmsteads of the area; these included Raise, Jollybeard and Lovelady Shield. Tenant farmers held a portion, or moiety, of each tenement; this formed the parcel of land in the vicinity of their farmstead (Fig 14). The wills and probate inventories of the parish from 1600 onwards, preserved in the archives of Durham University Library, reveal that a farmer's stock of cattle, sheep and horses was usually his most valuable moveable asset, worth far more than his cash reserves, clothing or household goods. An example from the farmstead of Annat Walls is the probate inventory of Thomas Walton, yeoman, dated 1672.[13] No value is given for his house or land but solely for his moveable goods, which came to a total of £30 6s 8d. They include his horse and clothing, valued at £5, eight cows at £12, five heifers at £6, four calves at £1, twenty sheep at £3 6s 8d, and the rest of his goods, described as 'Powder brasse & other household goodes', at a total of £3. The reference to powder suggests that Walton, along with many of his contemporaries, had an interest in mining as well as farming.

Surrounding the farmsteads was a wider landscape of dry stone walls and mining remains. Edmond Sandford described the area in the 1670s as a 'rich grassing ground, and great herds of cattle, and flocks of sheep', while Thomas Denton wrote in 1687 that the people 'live upon their Stocks; and convert most

Figure 14
The tenements and landholdings in the vicinity of Garrigill, from a map of 1778.
[© The National Archives, ref. MR1/252/1/6]

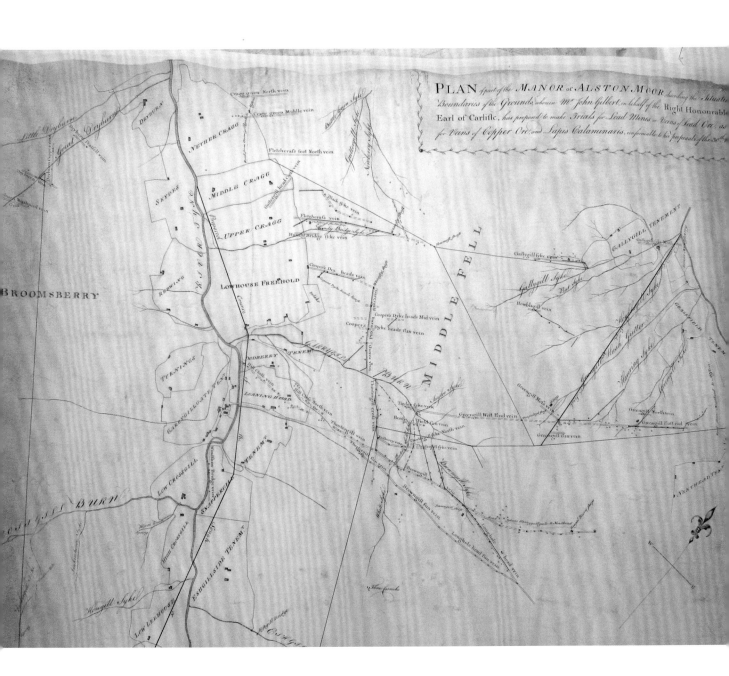

of their enclosures to Meadows, the place being too bleak and stony for Arable ground'.[14] Some arable cultivation continued into the early 18th century, suggesting that there may have been some efforts at land improvement at this date: in a court case of 1730, the tenants of farms at Bayles and Fairhill admitted that they had grown oats, barley and other grains since 1718, and they were consequently prosecuted for the non-payment of tithes.[15] Livestock, however, continued to be the major farming concern, even once the shielings fell out of use. A traveller to Cross Fell in 1747 saw the shielings and some lead workings abandoned and described the landscape around the fell as a place which was

> so much environ'd with large and extended morasses, rocks and mountains, that they exhibited a very frightful appearance, not the vestige of a house, except some old shields, where in former ages the people had resorted like the Asiatic Tartars to graze their cattle in summer, a practice now quite disus'd. There were a few sheep, but no deer, that we could see, tho' there are several on the heights.[16]

Even at this early date the writer found considerable romance and drama in the landscape, with its sink holes, burns and waterfalls set against a backdrop of sparse vegetation and deforestation, but the town of Alston was barely mentioned and only as the place from which Cross Fell could be reached.

The mining of lead and silver was of major importance in medieval Alston Moor, as it undoubtedly had been before. Some of the lead was particularly rich in silver, a highly valuable natural resource used for coinage and decorative metalwork, particularly jewellery, church plate and tableware. Lead had many uses, particularly in roofing and plumbing, and also in the manufacture of pewter. The minerals extracted from the parish travelled far afield: in the second half of the 12th century, lead from the Alston area was supplied for building work at Windsor for Henry II and also to the great monastery of Clairvaux in north-east France.[17] Although early lead and silver extraction has left much less trace on the landscape than later phases of mineral exploitation, mining was an important source of wealth to those who had the right to plunder the parish's natural resources. Documentary sources tell of the English crown selling leases of silver and lead mines, as well as royal protection being granted to the miners, throughout the Middle Ages.[18]

Early lead extraction took advantage of natural features which exposed a seam of lead on the surface, particularly in the beds of streams running off the fells. Waterways could be dammed in order to release a concerted, powerful rush of water – a process called hushing – which would expose more lead for the miners to dig out, creating even more pronounced valleys (Fig 15). Once a lead seam was identified, it could be further exploited by digging vertical shafts down to meet it; then the lead could be hacked out. Ring-shaped heaps

Figure 15
Aerial view of Redgroves Hush on Middle Fell,
showing the curving dam of the reservoir (bottom left)
at its head.
[20678/052]

of spoil, the detritus from digging these shafts, are an enduring feature of lead extraction in the area up to the early 18th century, often found in lines following a lead-bearing vein, known as rakes. By the end of the 17th century, miners had gunpowder in addition to hammers and spades to help them in their pursuit of lead ore (Fig 16). Extracted lead-bearing rock, or bouse, was then crushed by hammers, washed and sieved, in order to remove the maximum lead ore, or galena. The silver content of the galena could be got by smelting

Figure 16
Blasting, as depicted in an early 19th-century watercolour from a volume of drawings of lead mining in the North Pennines, dated between 1800 and 1820.
[© Science Museum/Science & Society Picture Library]

and the lead could then be moulded into stackable, uniform portions known as pigs. However, there is little evidence for smelting in Alston Moor before the 18th century.

Reiving and civil unrest

In the context of complex cross-border relations, Alston Moor stood in a precarious situation. Not only was it a place where large quantities of livestock, particularly cattle, were reared, but it was located just to the south of a highly troubled region, the much-debated Anglo-Scottish border. The area's constant oscillation between war and peace in the Middle Ages resulted in a Border society without effective taxation and legislation, and with families, or 'names', set against one another in mafia-like rivalries. This frequently manifested itself in internecine strife and widespread reiving (raids targeting livestock) on both sides of the Border. The three Marches (West, Middle and East) were established by England and Scotland from the end of the 13th century to police this lawless area, with the appointment to each of the Marches of a pair of Lord Wardens – one English, one Scottish – to mete out justice to transgressors.

Alston Moor lay just to the south of the southern border of the English Middle March; it was not a major centre for reiving activity, having no resident 'names', but it was close enough to Tynedale and the Scottish borders, and wild enough, to attract some fringe activity. Horses and cattle stolen from Teesdale were driven through the centre of Alston Moor in 1511 and horses were removed from the area by the Scots. When relationships soured still further between England and Scotland, Henry VIII declared war on Scotland in 1522; in June 1523, Sir William Hilton took some of his tenants from Alston Moor to join the attack on Kelso and other Border targets led by Lord Dacre and the Earl of Surrey.[19] The 16th and early 17th centuries saw some of the worst atrocities. In November 1595 three murders were committed in Alston Moor, much to the concern of the English Warden of the Middle March.[20] Disputes and raids were not merely cross-Border, however, but were as likely to be local. In 1555, for example, Sir Thomas Hylton [Hilton] complained to the Earl of Shrewsbury and the Council of the North about the action between his own tenants in Alston Moor and those of Lord Dacre arising out of a Scottish cattle raid.[21]

Early buildings in Alston Moor

Few traces remain of medieval buildings in Alston and in its outlying settlements, largely because growing prosperity and stability allowed people to replace antiquated dwellings with new structures on similar sites. This has also been the fate of the parish churches in Alston and in Garrigill. One early form of domestic building found in Alston Moor is the tower house, a defensible building type popular on both sides of the Scottish Border. Tower houses

Figure 17
Randalholme, the tower house to the north of Alston.
[BB99/02603]

Figure 18
High Lovelady Shield, showing the gable end of the earliest, lowest part of the house.
[DP155001]

provided compact, multi-storeyed accommodation and were strongly built of stone; their size could be easily varied according to their owners' means. The parish's best example is at Randalholme, to the north of Alston. The tower, of roughly square plan, was constructed over a stone-vaulted basement, with thick walls, several storeys and an intramural stair. There is much speculation as to its date, but it may have been built as late as the 16th century. Its present appearance, with sash windows and armorial plaque, owes much to the mid-18th century (Fig 17).

The majority of vernacular buildings before 1600, however, would have been low in height, perhaps of only one or one and a half storeys, built of rubble or turf, and almost certainly thatched with heather over a steeply pitched roof. Timber-framing, in an area denuded of forest by the early middle ages, was impractical. Archaeological evidence has been found of a possible longhouse, close to the Gilderdale Burn and Howgill Rigg. Its rough outline is clearly visible, but this outline presents few suggestions as to its internal arrangement, such as evidence of a cross passage which would have provided access to both the domestic accommodation and the byre. However, the outline alone suggests that the longhouse, a typical farmstead form, may have been prevalent in the area during the middle ages, as it was across much of northern and western England and Scotland.

Such a structure can be found embedded in the earliest part of the farmstead at High Lovelady Shield (Fig 18). The scar of one end of a rubble building is encapsulated within the only internal wall to remain standing in its entirety; it is one storey high, but with a ledge at eaves height to carry a floored attic. This building, of which this is the only trace, had a steeply pitched roof, steep enough to indicate heather thatch. The wall thickness, of under a metre, does not suggest any great defensibility. We cannot know from the evidence of this single surviving wall the extent or layout of the structure, nor its fenestration or pattern of doorways, but it was built over and around to form a squarish, two-storey building at the core of the farmstead, to which several further additions were applied in the 17th and 18th centuries.

Such insubstantial vernacular buildings were hard to defend during a raid on the area's valuable livestock – they were easily destroyed by fire or brute force. The construction of tower houses, a formidable response to aggression, required more time and financial investment, and so these were commissioned

Figure 19
The much rebuilt bastle at The Raw, near Hepple, Northumberland, which eventually gained a permanent exterior stair.
[DP135346]

Figure 20
The stone-vaulted byre and its original byre doorway, at The Raw, near Hepple, Northumberland.
[DP135347]

Figure 21
The tiny intramural stair next to the byre doorway at Craig Farm, near Hepple (top) and the trap door in the byre vault at Hole, Bellingham (above), both in Northumberland.
[DP155002, DP155003]

by those at the upper end of rural society who owned their own land and had a great deal at stake. However, those who still had property to defend but much smaller means with which to do it required a different response, one which led to the construction of a small, but strong, defensible building type: the bastle.

The bastle: a Border building type

The bastle was the most popular built response to Border instability, a building that could protect both human and animal life together, countering the dual threats of reiving and inclement climate. It is a building type frequently found on both sides of the Anglo-Scottish border, some of the best surviving examples being in Northumberland (Figs 19 and 20). It combined a safe place for a farmer's cattle with accommodation for his family, and it was built from the local sandstone rubble and reinforced at the corners with strong stone quoins. The bastle, built on a rectangular plan, consisted of a ground-floor byre for the cattle, with no windows, a handful of ventilation slits and a single doorway. Set above the byre on the first floor was a single room, occasionally subdivided, with a few small windows, a hearth set beneath a primitive chimney known as a smoke hood, and a doorway that could only be reached by a ladder. This was the sole space for human habitation and was used for living, cooking, eating and sleeping. Some additional sleeping or storage space may have been provided in a loft.

Defensibility was an important function of the bastle: in order to protect both human and animal occupants, the walls were usually around a metre thick, windows were kept to a minimum and the two doorways were provided with long slots into which large wooden bolts, known as drawbars, could be slid to secure them from the inside. Permanent external stairways to reach the first floor were generally avoided in favour of a ladder – this could be drawn up behind the family to make it even harder for attackers to reach the people inside. In rare cases in Northumberland, the bastle had an intramural stair, built between the inner and outer skins of the external wall, to provide a means of access between the byre and the first floor, as at Craig Farm, Hepple; more may have had just a ladder and a trap door, as at Hole, Bellingham (Fig 21).

The living space above could be protected still further by the construction of a stone barrel vault over the byre, as many Northumberland examples show. This feature is generally interpreted as protecting the people above from a fire in the event of the byre's security being overcome. Fire was one of the major weapons used by attackers, as the presence of so-called 'quenching holes' over some of the byre doorways demonstrates – people on the first floor could pour water directly down over the wooden byre door to hinder the attackers from burning it down prior to stealing the cattle.

Alston Moor was as susceptible to livestock raids as anywhere in northern Cumbria, Northumberland or southern Scotland – the beasts raised on the fells of the North Pennines represented a significant income for its tenant farmers, in an area where arable farming was confined to a small proportion of lower-lying ground. The building of the first bastles across the Borders during the late 16th and early 17th century was an attempt by some farmers to protect their most valuable property – their cattle – and their families; flocks of sheep would have to take their chance in a raid. The bastle thus represented an attempt to consolidate the Border farmer's precious assets; it kept those assets under one roof just as the longhouse had done, but in a more compact, defensible form. The bastle was not an instant response to the instability of the region, but by the early 17th century it was a useful type of farmstead, which could be found widely in the area, for those farmers who could afford to construct them.

Alston Moor's bastles

Alston Moor's bastles largely conform to the characteristics noted above. They are walled in rubble with large stone quoins at the corners, and dressed stone is used for the window and door surrounds, with a simple chamfer (about 5cm wide) framing each opening. Windows are frequently mullioned, with one or two vertical stone bars dividing up the window opening (Fig 22). The stone lintel of the byre doorway can be treated in various ways: it can have a straight, triangular or curved head and may be decorated with a date and the initials of the tenant farmer who had paid for the building work. Dates and initials became increasingly popular through the 17th, and into the early 18th, century; they were carved not only into door lintels but also over windows (Fig 23).

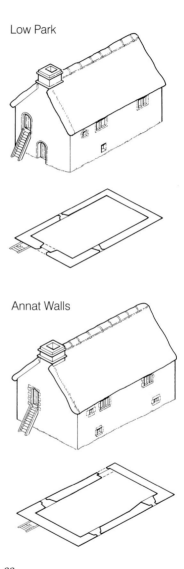

Low Park

Annat Walls

Figure 22
The earliest 17th-century phase of Low Park and Annat Walls, showing their similarity in plan and dimensions; their principal divergence is in the position of the byre doorway.

The first floor of a bastle was generally heated by a hearth against the gable wall, set under a smoke hood. Many traces of smoke hoods can be found across the parish, which is unusual in comparison to a very poor survival rate of this feature in the bastles of Northumberland. Smoke hoods were lightweight structures of timber and plaster which were positioned above the only hearth, backing on to one gable wall; the hood channelled the smoke up to the stone chimney on the gable apex. The chimney and the hood were supported on large stone corbels built into the thickness of the wall, many of which have survived; less evidence has been found of the pieces of wood which would have supported the structure from below (Fig 24). Roofs were supported by collared trusses, usually with a double-pegged collar and apex. Heather thatch was the preferred roofing material: the steep pitch associated with heather thatch can be seen in roof scars at High Lovelady Shield, Lower Crossgill and Blagill. The domestic accommodation could be subdivided into two rooms by a timber partition. The smaller of the two rooms was unheated and used for sleeping, while the larger of the two contained the hearth and smoke hood and was the principal living and cooking space (Fig 25).

Figure 23 (above)
Datestones from across the parish.
[DP154198, DP154192, DP154222]

Figure 24 (right)
Looking up the inner face of the gable wall at Low Park, where projecting stones were once used to support a smoke hood.
[DP109689]

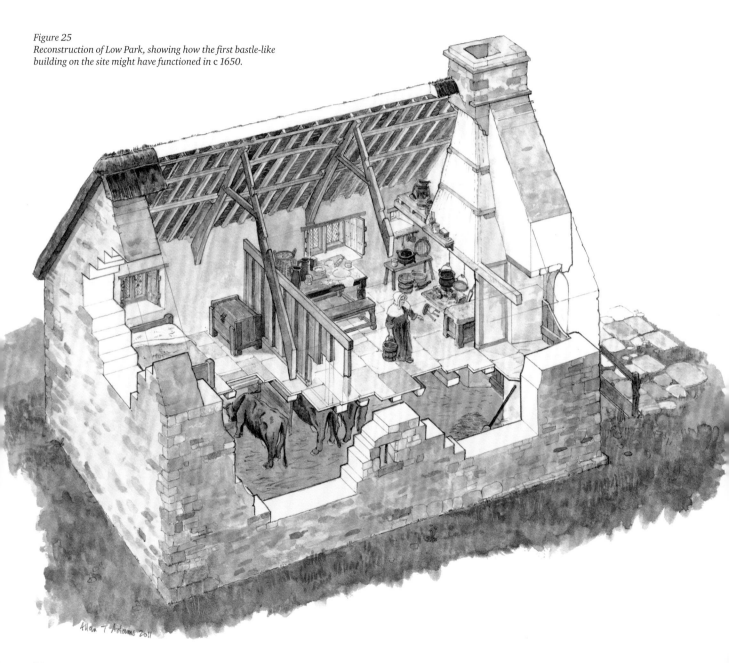

Figure 25
Reconstruction of Low Park, showing how the first bastle-like
building on the site might have functioned in c *1650.*

Figure 26
Large stone flags are laid on timber joists to form the floor between the byre and the living space at Annat Walls.
[DP109774]

The bastles of Alston Moor, however, differed in a number of respects. Where those of Northumberland and southern Scotland were often characterised by a stone-vaulted byre, most Alston Moor bastles have an upper floor carried by heavy timber beams and joists (Fig 26). There is a divergence in the placing of the first-floor doorway, too. Elsewhere, this is usually positioned about a third of the way along one of the two long walls, but many examples in Alston Moor concentrated all of their key features onto one gable wall. Here, the byre doorway was centrally positioned with a smoke hood and a chimney directly above it with the first-floor doorway set to one side, next to the hearth. Interestingly, the relationship between the first-floor entrance and the hearth is reminiscent of that found between the cross-passage and the house-part in longhouses, while the proximity of the ground- and first-floor entrances maintains as close a relationship between the living accommodation and the byre – a key characteristic of the longhouse – as the two-storey arrangement will permit. This combination of features has been seen across the parish, for example at Annat Walls, Middle Bayles and Low Park.

Why should Alston Moor have its own variant on a well-used building type? The inaccessibility of the parish may have encouraged its continuance, but could not have inspired its creation, for in most respects Alston Moor's bastles follow the layout and design seen in Northumberland. As to the choice of flagstones on timber joists over a stone barrel vault for the byre's ceiling, it may be that flagstones and timber were more easily obtainable in the parish compared to other areas of bastle construction. However, there may be a simpler explanation: in the long winter months, the bastles' occupants would have been glad to take advantage of the warmth created by the animals in the byre beneath them, warming their flagstone floor. Even as late as the mid-20th century, a former inhabitant of Annat Walls remembered that the rising heat from the cattle made a substantial difference to a family's comfort in the height of winter; a similar theory has also been associated with the longhouse plan.

Many of the long-established settlements may have acquired a bastle by the mid-17th century. Sometimes two or more were grouped together into tiny hamlets, such as at Loaning Head above Garrigill Bridge, and there is some evidence that their development might be kin-related. Most were built along the contours of the landscape in the manner of longhouses, though some were

Figure 27
The hamlet of Annat Walls, c 1900, showing the majority of the buildings running north to south along the contour, with the exception of the 1707-dated bastle in the foreground; this is now ruined and was built down the slope.
[© Carlisle Library, Cumbria County Council]

constructed across the contours (Fig 27). The bastle quickly superseded the older farmsteads, being such a significant improvement on the previous buildings, but, importantly, this continuity of site maintained the tradition of dispersed settlement in the area which is still so familiar and striking today. In 1687 Thomas Denton described the buildings and landscape of the parish, writing that 'the houses stand stragling all over the parish as if they were affraid one of another'.[22]

A good climate for building?

The construction of Alston Moor's bastles may have been stimulated by a decision by the then lords of the manor, the Hilton family, to assess and re-establish the leases held by their tenants. On the death of Sir William Hilton in 1600, a series of leases for 21 years were issued; then, in 1610 and 1611, Henry Hilton offered his lessees the right to buy a further lease for 1,000 years at the cost of

21 years' rent and a smaller annual fee, to become active when the 21-year lease expired at the end of 1621. In addition, the sum equivalent to 21 years' rent was to be paid every 21 years (Fig 28). This may have been part of the Hilton family's disengagement from the manor of Alston Moor – they may have needed to reform the land-holding system in order to raise money. In 1618, Henry Hilton mortgaged the manor to Sir Francis Radcliffe, 1st Baronet, of Dilston, Northumberland; this was eventually followed by the sale of the manor for £2,500 to Sir Edward Radcliffe, Sir Francis's successor, in 1629. At that date the manor included 120 acres of demesne land (a figure similar to

Figure 28
A detail of one of the 1,000-year leases. This one is between Henry Hilton and Thomas Crawford of Park, Alston Moor, and is dated 31 August, here written as the 'laste day of August', 1611.
[© The National Archives, ref. ADM 75/66]

that mentioned in the 1315 inquest), houses at Lowbyer and Mark Close, and a corn mill in Alston.[23]

Henry Hilton's mortgage and subsequent sale of the manor of Alston Moor was not to fund a profligate lifestyle nor to raise money for a marriage portion, as some commentators have thought. It appears to have been in preparation for an immensely generous bequest to be paid on his death, which occurred in 1641: he left £24 per annum to be paid for 99 years as charitable donations to 38 parishes in Durham, Surrey, Sussex, Middlesex and Newcastle upon Tyne, a sum which amounted to £912 a year. This staggering generosity, however, far exceeded both the £228 per annum to be paid to family and friends and the capability of the estate to raise the necessary funds. Eventually, payments to the parishes were renegotiated and lowered; the charity continued until 1739 while the Hilton family, gradually beggared by the bequest, sank to the rank of gentry.[24]

Just as the manor of Alston Moor was beginning to reorganise its leases, the accession of James VI of Scotland to the English throne as James I in 1603 spelled the beginning of the end of the tacit toleration of cross-Border conflict. The associated theft and knavery took many decades to be completely suppressed, however, and was then followed by the painful national upheavals of the Civil War. A troop of Parliamentarian cavalry sacked houses and took prisoners in Alston in 1643, while in 1652 Robert Whitfield of Randalholme had his estate confiscated by Parliament for his part in supporting the Royalist cause.[25] Horse-stealing remained prevalent, as petitions submitted to the Cumberland Quarter Sessions by aggrieved residents of Alston Moor in 1688, 1691, 1702 and 1704 show.[26] The area remained unsettled for quite a time: William Wallace, writing in 1890, described how his grandmother had told him that

> during her grandfather's time, the family was careful to arrange axes and other weapons at the head of their beds, in order to be in readiness to defend their property against the Scotch. The family were living at Annetwalls [Annat Walls] in 1726, and how long before that date I have not ascertained. The country was in a very unsettled state about the time of the rebellion of 1715.[27]

But for the yeomen of Alston Moor, the benefit of the 1,000-year leases and of lengthening periods of political stability was substantial. They acquired secure, long-term tenure, contributing to a rise in their social status and their ability and desire to invest in their land. This in turn led to the construction of more permanent and substantial farmsteads, the form of which reflected a continuing desire for defensibility and security at a time of immense unrest. Even once the need for defence declined, the rural population of Alston Moor was left with numbers of strongly built farmsteads which provided warmth and shelter from the elements, alongside security for men and beasts alike.

The role of Greenwich Hospital and the London Lead Company

Figure 29
The former Royal Hospital for Seamen, Greenwich, designed by Sir Christopher Wren between 1694 and 1700 but still under construction in the 1730s.
[BB96/07646]

In the early 18th century, as before, periods of instability were never far away. The upheavals of the Hanoverian succession in 1715 were felt strongly in Alston Moor, resulting in a momentous period of change. The then lord of the manor was James Radcliffe, 3rd Earl of Derwentwater, the grandson of the 1st Earl (himself the grandson of the Sir Francis Radcliffe of Dilston, who had bought Alston Moor from the Hilton family). Derwentwater was a notable Jacobite who, as one of the few ringleaders of the uprising against the Hanoverians to be caught, was tried and executed for his part in the rebellion against George I in 1716. After decades of legal wranglings, it was finally established that the greater part of his heirs' estates should be sequestrated; in 1735 those lands, including the manor of Alston Moor, were given by the government to the Royal Hospital for Seamen at Greenwich, where their revenues were intended to provide an income to complete the building and to contribute to the running of the institution (Fig 29).

For the first time, Alston Moor was not in the hands of a landed family: now the manor was run by, and for the benefit of, a London-based institution. The Commissioners of Greenwich Hospital, in order to run their new Alston Moor estate and safeguard their interests, appointed two Receivers and their first 'Moormaster', John Friend of Spency Croft. This enabled the estate to function much as it had under the Radcliffes: the Commissioners employed the Moormaster to negotiate leases for mines and the Receivers to deal with and to ensure the good governance of all other property. The Quaker-run London Lead Company, already a considerable presence in the area from the 1690s, became further involved between 1750 and 1765, when it bought mining leases from Greenwich Hospital on land in the Nent valley and extended its lease on Priorsdale, thus giving it greater access to the mineral wealth of Nenthead, Garrigill and the surrounding areas. Although some mines in Alston Moor were independently exploited, the London Lead Company was by far the largest operator in the area. They did not employ the majority of their workforce directly; groups of miners would make their own contracts with company agents in order to have the right to investigate and exploit a particular seam and would then receive payment at an agreed rate for any ore that was excavated.

The development of the bastles

There were many bastle-like farmsteads across the parish by 1700, and their compact form and single-cell plan with limited fenestration lent themselves admirably to additions over time. A bastle could be extended from either or both gable walls, a method which inevitably led to the development of the linear farmstead – so-called because the house and the working buildings are attached in-line – which is found so frequently in the parish. Typically clinging to the contours of the slope, the bastle could also be extended with an outshot on the uphill slope, providing better service accommodation for the living areas. This results in a mismatch of storeys, with the uphill elevation of a farmstead often presenting a single storey while the downhill side can have two or three, as the bastle terrace of Dryburn shows. Adding an outshot on the uphill side, however, would compromise any defensive aspect to the farmstead, but such additions usually post-date 1700 when the need for defensibility was already fading.

Indeed, an extended line of bastles often forms the core of the linear farmsteads which are to be found across the parish today. At Annat Walls itself, the much rebuilt central bastle was extended at both gable ends; the addition to the south formed an extension to the original bastle, but built onto the north gable was an entirely separate bastle house (Fig 30).

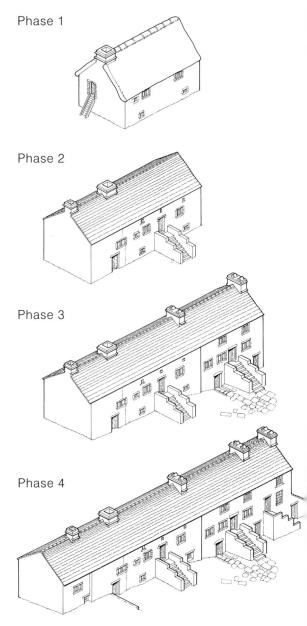

Phase 1

Phase 2

Phase 3

Phase 4

Figure 30 (opposite)
The phasing of Annat Walls, demonstrating the additive
quality of many bastle farmsteads in the area. For the
original fenestration of the 1735 part of the house,
see Figure 7.

Figure 31 (below)
Middle Park, near Raise, Alston.
[DP109696]

This northern addition is dated 1735 and retains all the main characteristics of the earlier form – a ground-floor byre and a first-floor doorway – while offering two good storeys of accommodation, as well as a lit attic space; it was itself later extended on the western, downhill side. Adding to the gable end of the bastle often resulted in the blocking of the original first-floor doorway. Consequently, both at Low Park and at Annat Walls, new doorways had to be made in the long elevation, changing the whole emphasis of the design. The extended houses were eminently adaptable: either the existing accommodation of the owner or occupier could be improved and enlarged, or a separate house could be provided either for rent or to house part of their extended family.

Linear farmsteads in Alston Moor do not always consist solely of bastle-like elements. At Hill House, Bayles, a two-storey addition, probably of the late 17th century, was built against the gable wall of an earlier bastle. This addition dispenses with the bastle form and provides living accommodation on two storeys. One wall incorporates a curved projection, housing a winder stair, and exhibits a number of chamfered window surrounds. This prosperous farmhouse also has a ground-floor fire window set under a smoke hood, the supports for which still survive. The ground floor of the two-storey wing was clearly intended for domestic use from the start rather than as animal accommodation, demonstrating an alternative farmstead layout to the traditional Alston Moor bastle was in use in the period. At Middle Skelgill a similarly sized 17th-century two-roomed wing was added to the gable end of an earlier single-cell house. From current research, however, such additions seem to be unusual and may reflect a rare period of affluence or tranquillity.

Houses with the living accommodation set over a byre continued to be built in Alston Moor into the 18th century and even beyond, but explicitly defensive features were abandoned and various refinements were introduced, both in newly built houses and in those earlier houses that were upgraded. Middle Park, a house of the late 18th century, is a good example of such a house-over-byre, with its ground-floor byre and single-storey house above, but it has thin walls, large windows and a distinct shortage of defensible features (Fig 31). In houses old and new, fireplaces with stone jambs and lintels gradually replaced the smoke-hooded hearth as the principal form of heating. At Low Park, for instance, the first floor of the house was subdivided, retaining the smoke hood for heating half the building while introducing a stone fireplace to heat the other half; the whole building was also extended to either side to give further heated rooms with byres beneath. A second storey of accommodation was often created by raising the eaves or adapting the roof space. The wider use of stone slates made possible roofs of a shallower pitch than had been required for heather thatch. Chamfering remained the principal means of decorating the stonework around windows and doors, although chamfers were smaller and more delicate than before. Mullioned windows remained popular into the middle of the 18th century, but the mullions were slimmer than those of preceding centuries. At South Loaning House, around 1750, slim mullions divide the pairs of sash windows that light a polite three-storey block which was built around the remains of a bastle, part of which is embedded in its western wall (Fig 32).

Figure 32
South Loaning House, a house with bastle-like origins clad in a smart, 18th-century façade.
[DP154243]

Figure 33
Chamfered and mullioned windows in the rear,
churchyard-facing elevations of two houses on
Front Street, Alston.
[DP154263, DP154264]

Alston takes shape

By the middle of the 18th century, Alston had already acquired much of its present form, with Front Street, the churchyard, The Butts and the market place at its core and Townhead and Townfoot at its extremities. The burn that flowed through the town was already supplying water power to a forge and two corn mills, but the area to the east of it was not yet developed into Back o' the Burn. The area to the south of the churchyard was developed into a market place surrounded by shops in the period around 1700; it had previously been thought of as a common, although commerce must already have been taking place there for many years. Its small size may suggest that this was a provisions market, with the trading of livestock being done elsewhere, for example on Fair Hill. The manor granted two licences, one in 1697 and the other in 1703, to build shops; these were described as structures to be put up 'upon the Comon' which should not exceed 10 yards long and 5 yards wide.[28] It is not known which are the exact plots to which these licences refer, but the dimensions are closest to those of the two properties (each consisting of a house over a shop) now called Cross View Cottage. The western house has a frontage onto the market place of about 5 yards 9 inches (4.8m), while the eastern house's frontage is 5 yards 33 inches (5.42m) wide; both have a depth back to the churchyard of around 8¼ yards (7.74m and 7.56m). All of the other plots in the vicinity of the market place today are much larger than the maximum of 10 by 5 yards mentioned in 1697. But in all cases, the depth of the plots indeed does not exceed the 10 yards specified in the documents. However, the question remains as to whether some of the buildings around the market place are in fact a little older, having encroached upon the common rather aggressively and thus prompted stricter regulation by the manor thereafter.

Most of the surviving vernacular buildings of the period are found on Front Street, in The Butts and around the market place and churchyard. The rubble-walled houses are largely two-storeyed although some have two and a half, three or even four storeys. They have distinctive chamfered door and window surrounds; the original window style appears to be squarish in shape, with larger ones divided by a central mullion (Fig 33). The houses on Front Street backing onto the churchyard display their older and more revealing elevations to the churchyard, with their Front Street elevations largely refaced

Figure 34
The churchyard-facing elevations of houses on Front Street, Alston.
[DP135367]

(Figs 34 and 35). At Lantern House, a small chamfered window lies just to one side of the projecting sweep of its central winder stair, suggesting that at this date the stair of these double-fronted three- and four-storey houses was centrally placed at the rear of the house, connected to the central door onto Front Street by a passage with a single room per storey to either side.

Many buildings retained the first-floor entry to the domestic quarters so prevalent in rural parts of the parish. Cross View Cottage, which overlooks the market place, is a house of about 1700 with chamfered windows in its rear elevation, refronted in the later 19th century to merge with its neighbour. This house was only one bay wide, with its front door offset to the right up a flight of steps; the original arrangement of the building may have been commercial premises on the ground floor with separately entered accommodation above. Numerous buildings in The Butts, on Front Street and in Kings Arms Lane have, or had, first-floor doorways: even those doorways and flights of steps long since dismantled and removed have left many traces in the rubble walls of Alston's houses. Interestingly, in this urban context as in the countryside, the tradition of first-floor living continued well into the middle of the 18th century. Stokoe House, situated in Alston's market place overlooking the market cross, is an excellent example of an early 18th-century house built over a stable. The original first-floor entrance had external steps to the first floor, shown by Fryer and Hilton's map of 1775, but these had disappeared by 1861 when the first Ordnance Survey map was published. The jambs of the first-floor doorway still survive above the present entrance to the ground floor; the steps were

Figure 35
The row of houses built against the churchyard with frontages onto Front Street and the market place.
[DP154230]

angled and brought the visitor to a large landing half the width of the building (Fig 36).

Only a handful of buildings buck the trend of first-floor living. Church Gaytes Cottage on Front Street, dated 1681, has a small window, complete with chamfered surround, on the ground floor (Fig 37). Internally, it lights the space near the hearth, acting as a fire window; on the other side of the entrance doorway, a chamfered two-light mullioned window illuminates the other ground-floor room. This appears always to have been a two-storeyed building

Figure 36a (above)
Stokoe House, a building with its main elevation fronting the Market Place, Alston.
[DP109737]

Figure 36b (left)
Cross section of Stokoe House.

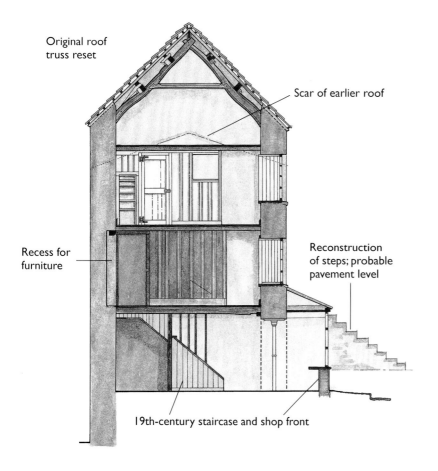

Original roof truss reset

Scar of earlier roof

Recess for furniture

Reconstruction of steps; probable pavement level

19th-century staircase and shop front

Figure 37 (above)
Church Gaytes Cottage (centre), Front Street, Alston.
[DP154220]

Figure 38 (above right)
Church View Cottage in The Butts, Alston, a two-storey
cottage above a basement; it has an original window in
its gable lighting the attic.
[DP154175]

with the entrance on the ground floor. In early 19th-century directories it was an inn, which may be a clue to why it differs from many of its neighbours. Church View Cottage, a two-storey house in The Butts facing the churchyard wall, has a partly decipherable date stone which places it in the 1690s. However, it sits on a substantial basement which must originally have been used for the storage of goods or as stabling, with no evidence of original heating and lighting, and which is entered by a door in a later outshot next to the gable wall. Making the best use of a sloping site, the main (first-floor) entrance is around the corner overlooking the churchyard, where the land is higher. One small, square, chamfered window survives in the gable of Church View Cottage with its original leaded glass and iron glazing bar; it once lit an attic room tucked under the substantial pegged and collared roof (Fig 38). It may from one side appear to be different from many houses in Alston, but the presence of the basement confirms that it functioned like them.

Figure 39
The Quaker meeting house at Townhead, Alston.
[DP154318]

Places of worship for dissenting denominations

Alston's earliest surviving buildings are all domestic and commercial premises, with one notable exception: the Quaker meeting house at the top end of Front Street, constructed in 1732 (Fig 39). With its neat rubble walls and chamfered window surrounds, it blends harmoniously with the local vernacular. It demonstrates how substantial the local Quaker community was in the 18th century, with the majority of the mining leases in the parish being held by the Quaker-run London Lead Company. This was the second meeting house put up by the Quakers: the first was built in 1724 at Wellgill near Nenthead, but no trace of this remains. These Quaker buildings followed in the footsteps of those of other dissenting groups: in 1689 the first Congregational chapel in Alston Moor was built at Loaning Head, on the lane above Garrigill Bridge. This chapel still survives, although converted to residential use in the 18th century and now renamed 'The Cottage'. Its rubble walls and large, inserted windows contribute to making this small, single-storey building appear quite domestic, with little hint of its origins (Fig 40). These new places of worship, however, were a sign of things to come: the Church of England was going to face stiff competition for the souls of the growing population of Alston Moor.

Figure 40
The former Congregational chapel at Loaning Head.
[DP154216]

3

The transformation of Alston Moor, 1770–1882

The last quarter of the 18th century saw the start of a period of tremendous change for Alston Moor. The mineral wealth of Alston Moor was increasingly exploited by the London Lead Company among others, bent on extracting as much lead ore as possible (Fig 41). Many people were drawn to the area because of the employment offered by the mineral industry and, in consequence, the population of the parish grew rapidly throughout the period, rising to its peak of nearly 7,000 in 1831. Alston, from being the market town of the area, became a centre for collecting and transporting the processed lead ore, as well as providing a home to many people involved in the lead industry and serving as the administrative heart of the parish. Nenthead and Garrigill, once concerned with agriculture and smaller-scale mining, grew to accommodate much of the mining-related workforce and, in the case of Nenthead, much of the mineral processing too. Individual farmsteads were not immune from change, proving their adaptability and flexibility in the face of a changing world, including a landscape transformed by enclosure and improvements in agriculture. The confidence of the area was high, even in the face of fluctuating lead prices; with better roads and the arrival of the railway, modern Alston Moor was born.

Transport and travel

Alston Moor's isolation from major centres of population and manufacturing, and its involvement in the production of so heavy a commodity as lead, made it more than usually dependent upon good communication networks. Travel into and around the parish, whether for goods or people, had always been difficult. Alston Moor had long been connected by road to Hexham and Carlisle via the South Tyne valley and to Penrith via the Hartside Pass, but during the later 18th century turnpike trusts were set up to improve those roads and a new road was built to connect Alston with Weardale. The turnpike trusts were united in 1823 and John McAdam, who was an adviser to Greenwich Hospital, was brought in to improve the turnpike roads by eliminating steep gradients and difficult curves. McAdam stated in 1823 that the roads 'are altogether the worst that have yet come to my knowledge ... the work has been executed in the most slovenly careless manner'.[29] McAdam's scheme of 1823 for the

Figure 41
The level into Haggs Mine, Nentsberry.
[DP143584]

Commissioners of Greenwich Hospital created a series of new high-quality roads that criss-crossed the whole of the North Pennines, linking Alston with Penrith, Hexham and Brampton, to Teesdale via Garrigill and to Weardale via Nenthead.[30] These roads reduced travel times and haulage costs between the principal lead seams high in the Nent and South Tyne valleys, the main settlements and more distant markets, increasing the efficiency of industrial transport in advance of the railway and underpinning the 1820s economic boom (Fig 42). Traditionally, lead ore had been brought out of the mines to be processed, then brought to Alston by pony- or donkey-trains, known locally as galloways, following paths over the fells. The galloways also transported wooden props back up to the mines for the construction of the levels (Fig 43). But as lead production increased, so too did the use of horse-drawn railways; these connected the mines of the Nent valley with Nenthead, and Nenthead with Alston.

Alongside this region-wide investment, the London Lead Company built a complementary network of major roads between 1820 and 1830, under the direction of mining agents Robert and Joseph Stagg, specifically to link its North Pennine mining operations between Brough and Middleton, and Garrigill and Alston, as well as collaborating in the wider regional schemes of the Greenwich Commissioners. Including work on improving minor routes and

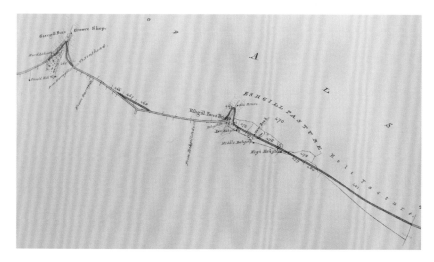

Figure 42
Revised road alignments, drawn in red, for the area around the Garrigill Burn and Ashgill, as proposed in 1823.
[© CAS, ref. QRZ 10, map 5]

Figure 43
Galloways at work in the North Pennines.
[© Science Museum/Science & Society Picture Library]

crossroads throughout the 19th century, a total of £12,500 was spent between 1815 and 1865 on company roads that directly benefited the mining industry.[31] This was a specifically economic investment in lowering the cost of lead transportation and increasing the productive time of mine agents, though there were, naturally, knock-on benefits for the local population in terms of lower prices for food and other supplies.[32] Long after the railway reached Alston, the roads of the 1820s and 1830s continued to provide many essential routes, especially across the moors and linking scattered mines to the railhead at Alston, and they were well maintained as a result. The County Road Surveyor declared in 1879 that Alston Moor's roads were 'the best managed … I ever had the pleasure of looking over'.[33]

Of more lasting significance was the coming of the railway. Indeed, by its architectural presence alone, Alston's station acted to reinforce the civic and industrial confidence of the period. The Newcastle & Carlisle Railway completed their Alston branch from Haltwhistle in 1852, using the services of Newcastle-based architect Benjamin Green. Green created at Alston a set of station buildings that were stylistically reminiscent of his work on the grander east coast mainline, drawing on a refined, domestic idiom of Tudor inspiration, with hood-moulded and stone-mullioned windows, and a roofline graced with tall grouped chimneys and gables topped with ball finials (Fig 44). Snecked rubble masonry was used as the principal facing material, complementing the rustic textures of the local vernacular. Alongside the passenger facilities, the terminus at Alston included a large goods yard and associated buildings designed with the substantial local trade in minerals – and other heavy cargo such as stone and coal – in mind. In total, the combination of stone and coal sidings could accommodate 300 wagons, a considerable capacity, but one that was necessitated by the volume and diversity of the industrial output surrounding this single railhead. The area immediately surrounding the station estate directly to the north-west of Alston town centre was a crucial transport node where the turnpikes to Hexham and Weardale converged. It was also close to the mouth of the Nent Force Level and the site where tramways and an aerial ropeway conveyed stone from quarries at Newshield and Blagill. The railway

Figure 44
Alston station. The arrival of the railway brought hitherto unthought-of connections to Alston Moor.
[DP154233]

was largely immune from the snows which periodically blocked the moor roads, providing an all-weather link with the outside world; its eventual closure in 1976 was greatly lamented.

The investment in roads and rail created a useful and highly visible legacy well beyond the lifetime of the lead industry. Other infrastructure projects, perhaps equally important for the lead industry, are less prominent in today's landscape. The Nent Force Level was largely completed in 1839, barring some later extensions. Though it failed in its original aim of opening up rich new lead seams, it proved useful as a means of transport, with horses drawing canal boats through the broad tunnel to remove spoil from intersecting levels along the route, and to drain water from the mining networks. For a while, the Nent Force Level also served the enterprising tourists who were starting to explore the area; they could enjoy the eerie experience of an underground, torch-lit journey by boat. Across heavily mined areas such as Nenthead, tramways could be found which linked underground levels with dressing floors and spoil heaps on the surface, but these proved an ephemeral presence, detectable now, if at all, only as earthworks.

The landscape and settlements of lead mining

The 18th century saw several key developments in lead extraction and processing. Hushing continued to be used, but mostly for the initial exploration for new lead-bearing veins. Where ore had for centuries been extracted via vertical shafts, now horizontal levels or galleries were created as the rock along the vein was removed. This had the dual benefit of linking the shafts together underground while creating a tunnel which could be used for access or for drainage. The entrances to the levels from the face of the hillside were often architecturally treated and given a stone surround; they are some of the most evocative traces of lead mining of the period (Fig 45). The significance of the Nenthead area to the mineral industry was recognised by the epic design and construction of the Nent Force Level, designed to open up new lead seams while draining those that were already working.

Spoil from the mines could be either left in worked-out levels or brought to the surface, where it was formed into dumps, often finger-shaped, such

Figure 45
Entrance to some of the mining levels, at Haggs Mine, Nentsberry, and the Galligill Syke Mine at Nettle Hall.
[DP143585, DP155004]

as those that line the riverside at Nenthead and at High Lovelady Shield (Fig 46). Once the ore was brought up to the surface, it was crushed and washed to separate the galena from the rock. Up to the end of the 18th century, the partnerships of miners who had extracted the ore were also responsible for washing it, but in the early 19th century, water-powered washing floors were introduced and were managed directly by the companies, such as that built at Rampgill near Nenthead in 1818 by the London Lead Company.[34] The ore was then smelted by applying immense heat to the galena: this resulted in a liquid that was poured into moulds to form pigs, making the lead transportable. The Company had a smelt mill at Nenthead by the 1770s, with two further mills built in the vicinity of Garrigill: one at Beldy (which survives today, converted to a corn mill, then to a house), the other at Tynehead.

Garrigill expanded considerably in this period. The 1820 Enclosure Award map shows Garrigill as a group of farmsteads (Gatehead, Gatefoot and Ivy House) with no green, a few cottages and a funnel of tracks leading up to Alston, the South Tyne valley and the high fells (Fig 47). The rows of cottages which now link the farmsteads are largely not shown on the map; nor is the group of late 18th-century houses on the east side of the bridge. There, Bridge House and its neighbour display three full storeys while The Shieling and the adjoining Four Pines both have two good storeys with a third tucked up under the eaves. The omission of key dwellings may suggest that the lack of a green is also an aberration. Ivy House, the most substantial house in Garrigill, appears to have been constructed in the mid-18th century as a farmhouse to an existing farmstead (a date stone of 1694 has been reused as a lintel in a 19th-century outshot). Its symmetrical elevation with sash windows and shallow-pitched roof adjoins a tall barn; the approach to the house is dignified by the substantial rusticated gate piers and forecourt walling (Fig 48). The village was the centre of life for many of the scattered farmsteads and hamlets of the South Tyne valley. Much of the lead industry in the Garrigill area was clustered around Tynehead, 2½ miles to the south: this distance made many people dependent on the services that Garrigill could offer, namely for places of worship, schools, public houses and the smithy.

But the area most affected by the rapid industrialisation of the parish during the late 18th and early 19th centuries was Nenthead. In 1820, maps show two similarly sized settlements on either side of the river Nent:

Figure 46
A finger dump next to the ruined farmstead at High Lovelady Shield.
[DP154194]

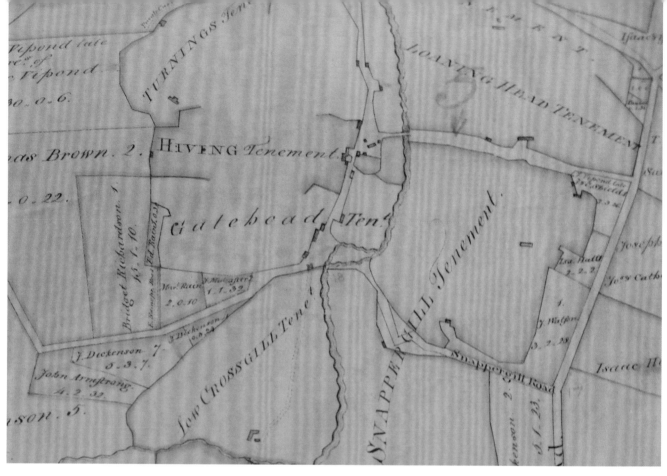

Figure 47
Garrigill, as shown on the 1820
Enclosure Award map.
[© CAS, ref. QRE 1/108]

Figure 48
Ivy House, Garrigill, a farmstead
substantially rebuilt in the later
18th century with a large in-line barn
to one side.
[DP154206]

Overwater on the south-west bank and Nenthead to the north-east (Fig 49). They were not yet linked by a road bridge, just by a network of pathways and tramways. To some extent, Overwater was the more conveniently situated of the two settlements for the mineral extraction industry, positioned as it was between the Rampgill mining complex and the river. This may account for the building of terraced houses of two and three storeys in Overwater, such as Dene Terrace, in some cases on rather small plots, in a manner suitable for the mass housing of a large number of miners and their families (Fig 50). These houses are rubble-built with sash windows and a shallow pitched roof; they are currently mostly rendered or painted. Nenthead, on the other hand, at this date followed the local rural pattern of dispersed settlement, with houses built in the bastle tradition along what was at that time its main thoroughfare,

Figure 49
The 1820 Enclosure Award map shows the embryonic Nenthead, with built areas shown around the Row (to the east), Whitehall (north of the Row) and Overwater (to the west).
[© CAS, Ref. QRE 1/108]

Figure 50
Houses in Overwater, with the three-storeyed examples
dating from around 1800.
[DP154134]

The Row. Overwater, then, was the first part of the area to be developed in direct response to the proximity of the Nenthead mines and processing areas. The two settlements lay together at the centre of a considerable network of tracks and tramways which had grown organically to link the entrances to the lead mines with the areas where the minerals were washed, crushed and processed and where many of the mineral workers lived.

Mine shops and accommodation adapted for miners

Garrigill and Nenthead, with Overwater, housed many people working in the mines of Alston Moor, but they could not provide for the entire mining population which was rapidly increasing throughout the later 18th and early 19th centuries. Novel ways were found to accommodate the newcomers, such as the mine shop, which provided accommodation for miners over a ground floor which was used for storing mining equipment or as a smithy. These mine shops were often built for workers at the remoter mines and were frequently situated right outside a level into the mine, which was entered through a stone entrance next to the shop. They provided overnight accommodation during the week for miners who lived further away from the lead seams – they would return home at weekends, no doubt relieved to be away from the bunkhouse-style conditions. The buildings were utilitarian, like the simple, plain building erected immediately adjacent to the stone entrance to Haggs Mine, near Nentsberry, for housing miners above a smithy. Other two-storey examples include Carr's Shop (built around 1815) and Hodgson's High Level Shop at Nenthead Mines, as well as the Blackburn mine shop at the entrance to one of its levels on Rotherhope Fell.

Farm incomes benefited not only from the growing market for produce but also from the increased demand for mine labour and for accommodation close to the mines. As mineral extraction boomed, the farmsteads became ever more crowded with people earning their living from the mines; some farmers rented or sold part of their property to miners while others had family members who were employed in the industry. As R W Bainbridge, chief agent of the London Lead Company, reported to a select committee in 1857:

> the population is so mixed up, the farming with the mining population, that they are almost all as one; it is scarcely possible to go into a family occupying half an acre in Alston Moor or Teesdale, without finding that one or more members of the family are workmen employed in the mines.[35]

Annat Walls, a farmstead which had achieved its fullest extent as two separate and substantial houses by the middle of the 18th century, was occupied by four households in the middle of the 19th century, most of which were involved in mineral extraction. Chimney stacks were inserted into previously agricultural and thus unheated spaces, bringing them into residential use, a pattern which was also followed extensively in the town of Alston.

Impressive evidence for an early 19th-century mining and housing operation remains at Nettle Hall, a farmstead in Galligill (Fig 51), situated on the southern side of the Nent valley to the north-west of Nenthead, close to the Galligill burn. Earthworks in the surrounding area show that this part of the hillside had already been exploited for lead mining in the preceding century. Then, in the early 19th century, the Galligill Syke Mining Company invested in further exploitation of the lead seams around the burn, with several adits, or levels,

Figure 51 (opposite top)
The farmstead of Nettle Hall.
[DP072081]

Figure 52 (opposite bottom)
The former reservoir in the mining complex above
Nettle Hall.
[DP155005]

Figure 53 (below)
The mine shop at Nettle Hall.
[DP072083]

Figure 54 (below right)
The kitchen fireplace in one of the early 19th-century
additions to Nettle Hall.
[DP072092]

running into the hillside high above the farmstead via stone entrances. Finger dumps were created from the piles of waste brought out of the adits. A small-scale washing and dressing area for the ore lay between the entrances to the levels and the farmstead, with a system of aqueducts and reservoirs to provide a constant water supply to the site (Fig 52). A mining complex such as this, just under 2 miles from the centre of Nenthead and 3½ miles from Alston, needed to provide some form of accommodation for miners from more distant localities. Consequently, a mine shop was built next to the farmstead, providing heated accommodation on the first and second floors to accommodate workers employed in the mine (Fig 53). The lack of fireplaces on the ground floor suggests that this space was intended for use as storage. At a similar date, Nettle Hall's 17th-century bastle range was extended several times and improved to enable it to be occupied by multiple households (Fig 54). This included the addition of a large room with a sizeable fireplace on the first floor, with its own flight of steps, designed as a self-contained, single-roomed dwelling. Mid-19th-century census returns confirm that many of Nettle Hall's households were employed in the mining industry.

The development of Alston

In 1775, the town of Alston was surveyed by John Fryer and Joseph Hilton (Fig 55). The resulting map shows that the historic core around Front Street, Townfoot, Townhead and The Butts was still the heart of the town. Archways between the houses of Front Street led to a number of tight lanes and courts. Indeed, the town was not much larger than it had been in the preceding century (Fig 56). The adaptation of much of the vernacular housing stock, with the conversion of basements into domestic spaces rather than workshops, stabling or storage, such as at Stokoe House, and the heightening of some buildings to provide additional accommodation, kept the town small, centralised and compact. Many houses in the heart of Alston, particularly in Townfoot, appear to date from the later 18th century, but the 1775 map suggests that many have older origins than their elevations might indicate. The stream was a dominant factor in the area to the east of the high end of Front Street, powering two large corn mills; one of these, High Mill, still survives. Back o' the Burn, a road following the line of the stream that combined housing with light industry (such as slaughter houses), is not shown, proving that it was not built up until later in the 18th century (Fig 57). Thomas Pennant made a tour to Alston only two years before Fryer and Hilton produced their map. He described Alston as a 'mine, and market-town, consisting of a number of small houses covered with flags, built irregularly, and extending lengthways up the side of a hill'.[36]

The Fryer and Hilton map reveals the prevalence of Alston's most typical vernacular feature: the external staircases which led to first-floor doorways, similar to the bastle tradition in the surrounding rural area. Relatively few functioning examples are to be found today, mostly in Front Street and around the market place, but they have left plenty of evidence, especially in areas of the town such as The Butts and Back o' the Burn where elevations have been renovated instead of rebuilt. A typical example would be Brook House in Back o' the Burn, of late 18th-century appearance: it exhibits a blocked first-floor doorway above the window to the right of the present entrance. The blocked doorway in the first floor of Arboreal Sunset View in The Butts carries the datestone 'T B 1752', conferring a higher status on that floor than the one below; the presence of an external stair is confirmed by the Fryer and Hilton map,

Figure 55 (above)
Detail of the title of the Fryer and Hilton map of Alston, 1775.
[© CAS, ref. DX 154/3]

Figure 56 (opposite)
The Market Place and Townhead, from the Fryer and Hilton map of Alston, 1775.
[© CAS, ref. DX 154/3]

Church Yard

Vicarage Croft

Market Place

Mill

Croft

Garden

Hundy Hall Field

School

with the steps running to the right-hand side of the building (Fig 58). The map's key tells us that a Thomas Bateman was the occupier at the date of the map, possibly the 'TB' of the datestone.

The retention of separate entrances to the lower and upper parts of buildings and external stairs serving the latter kept Alston's building stock adaptable and flexible in both function and layout, which may be part of the reason why many external stairs were retained for so long. Ground floors could continue to be used for stalling beasts, storing goods or running a shop or workshop, or they could be adapted to provide separate dwellings. Alston itself is situated on an extremely steep gradient and the topography of the town is such that buildings have to take significant account of dramatically sloping sites, requiring basements or ground works to provide a level building platform for the house above (Fig 59).

Alston's vernacular building traditions did not impress the visitor. Seen through the eyes of Eric Svedenstierna, a Swede who toured Britain in 1802–3, it was a 'small and badly built town, inhabited mainly by miners and other workers employed in the lead smelting works'.[37] However, Alston's tiny elite,

Figure 57 (opposite)
Aerial photograph of Alston, looking north to the market place. It shows the Back o' the Burn (also known as Overburn) curving south-eastwards away from Front Street on the line of the stream.
[20682/026]

Figure 58 (right)
Arboreal Sunset View, a house dated 1752, in The Butts, Alston. The blocked first-floor doorway is clearly visible above the present front door.
[DP154171]

Figure 59 (far right)
This house at the Townfoot end of Front Street demonstrates a typical response to Alston's steep gradient, with first-floor entrance, external stairs, and an extensive basement.
[DP154366]

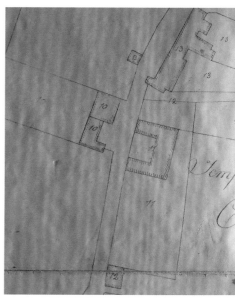

Figure 60
Alston House, as it is today and as depicted by Fryer and
Hilton as no. 11 on their map.
[© CAS, ref. DX 154/3, and DP154127]

and a few others, occupied houses more in tune with the symmetry and proportionality of the later 18th and early 19th century. Alston House, south of the
junction between Front Street and Townfoot and now a hotel (Fig 60), was
depicted by Fryer and Hilton as a U-shaped building with its courtyard facing
Townfoot; its wings are no longer in evidence as a result of rebuilding. In contrast to the rubble walling found in much of the parish, it is fronted with the
finest ashlar in the area and indeed is the only example of this from before
1800. Temple Croft, south of the vicarage, has 17th-century origins, with
chamfered and mullioned windows but also a solid 18th-century house
attached by an archway. The last of the larger houses is Laufran House on Front
Street, the former vicarage of *c* 1812, built by Greenwich Hospital to replace an
older vicarage after it had been declared to be in extremely poor condition.
Some smaller houses stylistically aped their larger neighbours, as the principal
elevation of Orchard House, Townfoot, demonstrates. Like most Townfoot
houses, it probably has earlier origins than its appearance might suggest. It
presents a regular, symmetrical elevation to the town, but an irregular elevation to the South Tyne river, complete with an arched stair window of the late

18th or early 19th century with Gothic-style glazing (Fig 61). Back Garth, a house in The Butts dated 1721 but used in the 19th century as an inn, also demonstrates a similar leaning towards proportionality, though not symmetry, in its street elevation. The dated door surround, however, is rusticated, a feature which was to recur in Alston well into the 19th century.

The most substantial building in the town was the church of St Augustine (Fig 62). The medieval church, long outgrown by the massive population increase, was declared by the Archdeacon of Northumberland in 1763 to be 'so ruinous in every part that it can never be effectually repaired'.[38] However, despite the rebuilt church and the sprinkling of larger, grander houses, visitors still failed to find the town attractive and up to date: Jollie's *Guide* of 1811 stated: 'There are some tolerable houses about Aldston; but buildings, in general, though formed of stone, and covered with slate, are rather mean and disagreeable.'[39] Efforts began to make Alston a better place to transact business, as befitted a town that lay at the heart of a major and lucrative industry, and to

Figure 61
Houses on Townfoot, Alston, with Orchard House in the centre.
[DP154218]

Figure 62 (opposite)
An early 19th-century watercolour of Alston, showing
St Augustine's church as built by Smeaton.
[© CAS, ref. DX 16]

Figure 63 (right)
A detail of the 1823 road proposals by McAdam and
Meaden, showing the proposed new market place
for Alston.
[© CAS, ref. QRZ 10, map 1]

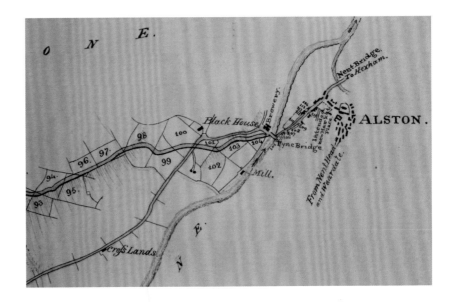

make it look more attractive. The market place was steep, curved and narrow in places, with the subsidiary Potato Market a little higher up Front Street – it was a picturesque arrangement born of long usage, but it was not, perhaps, the most practical site for the town's market. Several of the McAdam road maps of 1823 show an 'Intended New Market Place', to be situated at the junction of Townfoot and Front Street.[40] Those intentions may have encompassed some degree of levelling, to make a reasonably flat, or at least regular, site for the new market (Fig 63). The plan was also mentioned by Sopwith in 1833:

> It has been proposed to make a new market-place on the site of the Vicar's Croft, a small field in the lower part of the town, the completion of which, and the erection of some buildings on a uniform plan, would greatly improve the appearance of the place.[41]

The Vicar's Croft is Vicarage Croft, a large, rectangular parcel of land marked on the 1775 Fryer and Hilton map of Alston, surrounding the vicarage (now the site of Laufran House) and stretching down to Townfoot. Although this plan never came to fruition, it may be no coincidence that the site was later

Figure 64
Monument View, Townfoot, Alston.
[DP154154]

selected for the town hall and, later, the Walton Memorial, maintaining it as a focus for civic endeavour and achievement.

The vast influx of newcomers to the parish, lured by the burgeoning lead industry, had enormous consequences for Alston Moor, but interestingly the town of Alston did not see a corresponding boom in house building. The mid-19th-century censuses show that the town of Alston was bursting at the seams, with miners and their families crowded into houses all over the town, as they had been from the late 18th century. Those flexible ground-floor spaces, separated from the domestic areas above, were easily adapted: the insertion of a fireplace transformed previously uninhabitable parts of buildings into rooms to be let to miners and their families. These large fireplaces, with monolithic stone jambs and lintels, housed cast-iron ranges for cooking and the heating of water and mostly date to the decades around 1800. Monument View on Townfoot, originally a pair of houses built on the site of Alston's earliest Methodist chapel, has several ranges still *in situ*, dating from the time when it contained four separate households (Fig 64). At Stokoe House in the Market

Place, the ground floor first gained a large fireplace around 1800, and then a sink, creating a self-contained single-roomed dwelling in the space where the stable, then a shop, had once been; the roof was also raised to create an additional storey (Fig 65). This house, once designed for a single family, could now house two or three households. Although some buildings were constructed in the town in the first half of the 19th century, it is interesting that much of Alston's development concentrated on reusing the existing building stock instead of creating purpose-built suburbs on the fringes of the town.

Not surprisingly in a period of falling population, there was little residential development in Alston Moor, either private or speculative, after the high-water mark of the lead industry was passed. Indeed, in the parish as a whole, Wallace estimated that 344 houses had been abandoned, pulled down or converted to other uses between 1861 and 1881 alone.[42] The most substantial new development in Alston can be found in Croft Terrace, known as Church Terrace in the 19th century (Fig 66). This is a single row of two-storey houses, of varied size and plan, built in coursed rubble on a parcel of land (named Church Croft in 1775) to the north of the parish church. It first appears in the 1861 census and must have been recently built; at that date it was housing affluent members

Figure 65 (above)
Early 19th-century fireplace in the ground-floor room, originally built as a stable, at Stokoe House.
[DP109740]

Figure 66 (right)
Croft, previously Church, Terrace, Alston.
[DP154156]

of Alston's society, such as the families of agents to the coal and brewing trades. Another rarity is Albert House in the Garrigill Road area of Alston, a three-storey mid-19th-century townhouse with considerable pretensions. For the social levels below this, it was far more common to see the refronting or remodelling of older buildings, such as some of the houses around the market place in Alston. Cross View, for example, has an ostensibly late 19th-century elevation complete with barge-boarded gables which disguises a complex building history dating back to around 1700 (Fig 67).

In Raise, a small settlement to the west of Alston proper, an informal suburb of villa-like houses was gradually built from the 1820s onwards around a handful of earlier farmsteads. Although the number of houses developed here before 1900 is not large, there is evidence to suggest that this was more than a random accretion of high-quality houses on the outskirts of the town and more

Figure 67
Cross View, as seen from the market place, Alston.
[DP154143]

akin to a planned villa suburb. This sense is most acute on Raise Bank, the modern A689 road rising out of Alston on the west side of the South Tyne river, where a collection of houses with service outbuildings cluster together with a formality of plan that suggests a concerted programme of development. Here, the two principal houses, Raise Park and The Raise (which map evidence suggests were built around farmstead-like cores), are situated either side of the road with long, symmetrically arranged driveways sweeping up from roadside gates with flanking quadrant walls.

The London Lead Company at Nenthead

The London Lead Company had been working in the Nenthead area for many decades before they expanded the smelt mill and built a house for their agent there in 1753. From 1792, however, they sold their interests in Wales and Derbyshire to concentrate their efforts on Alston Moor and neighbouring Teesdale. Their investment in infrastructure, such as the Nent Force Level, the dressing floor at Rampgill, and the roads and wagon railways around Nenthead, was equalled by that in the landscape, where large tracts of trees, mostly Scots pine and larch with some oak, were planted in order to provide much-needed timber for the mines. Their greatest and most enduring investment, however, was to come in Nenthead itself with the building, from 1825, of 35 cottages for their smelters, 'overmen' (overseers) and senior members of the company, alongside institutional buildings to provide for the practical, educational and spiritual needs of the growing population. The miners themselves were already living in Overwater and in farmsteads in the Nenthead area – the new development did not include any provision for their accommodation, although a further three rows of four houses for miners were planned but not built. The new Nenthead was in many respects a model village expressing the aims and ethos of the Quaker-run company, with higher standards of domestic accommodation and a range of social amenities for employees outside their working hours. The amenities included a clock tower, market hall, school and chapel, creating an entire apparatus to support the higher standards of accommodation provided. The extent and nature of the new village are outlined clearly in plans drawn up in 1828 after the scheme's completion (Fig 68).

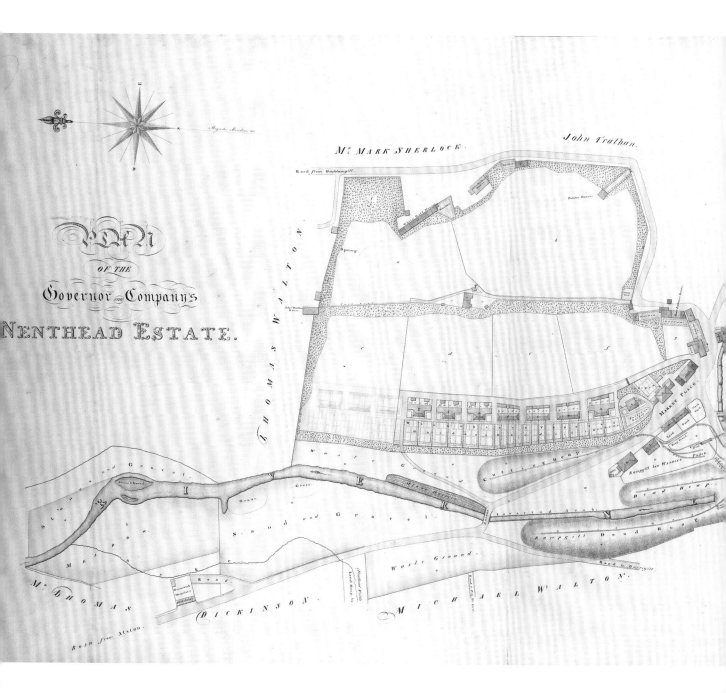

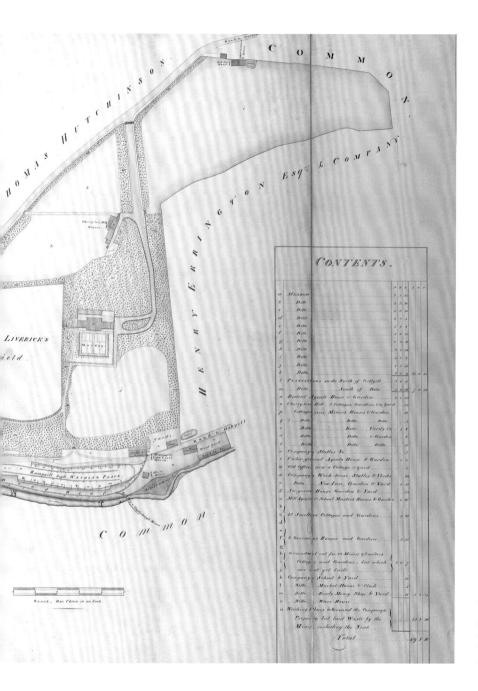

Figure 68
The London Lead Company's plan for the development of Nenthead, 1828. The three rows of houses on the western end of Hillersdon Terrace were never built.
[© NIMME, ref. 3410/LLC/Plans/2/3]

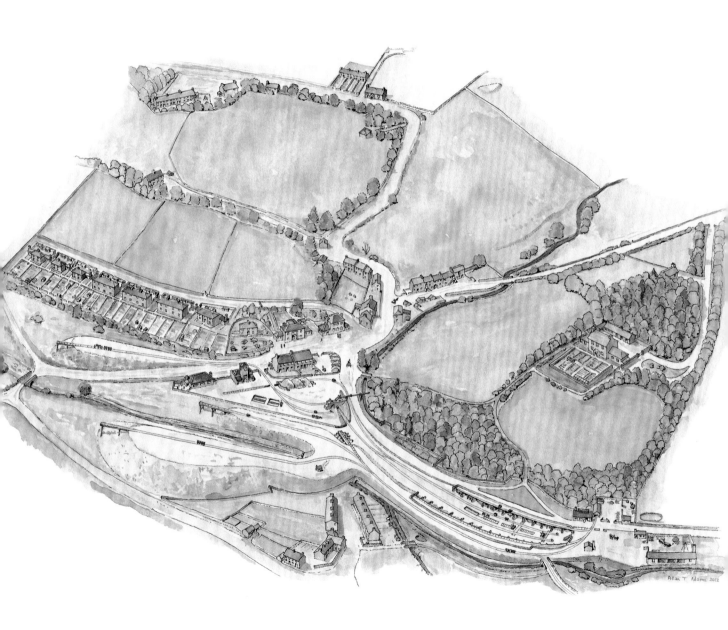

Hillersdon Terrace is the planned street at the heart of the London Lead Company's development, consisting of a sequence of seven housing blocks extending along the valley side overlooking the river. The blocks vary in size and arrangement of accommodation: a detached house for the surgeon, semi-detached houses for the mill agent and school master, one-bay terraced houses in rows of four for the smelters, and a semi-detached house of a spacious double-pile plan and a projecting rear wing housing a full range of services for the overseers (Fig 69). Unusually, the principal elevations and the carved stones announcing Hillersdon Terrace face down the valley towards the Nent rather than the lane (later Vicarage Terrace) behind. There are large gardens at the front of each house, with space for extensive cultivation and perhaps even the raising of poultry and pigs. At the rear, abutting the lane, tidily arranged spaces and outbuildings such as coal sheds and privies reflect the imposition of higher sanitary standards. The houses were designed within the prevailing vernacular style and with local materials (Fig 70).

It is clear that these dwellings were an improvement on previous accommodation in the area. A Dr Peacock, visiting Nenthead in 1864 in order to draw up a parliamentary report on the living and working conditions of miners, discussed the smelters' cottages in particular:

Figure 69 (opposite)
Reconstruction of Nenthead as it might have been around 1850, based on the London Lead Company's plan of 1828 and the 1st edition OS map of 1861.

Figure 70 (right)
A pair of houses in Hillersdon Terrace, Nenthead, designed to house 'overmen'.
[DP154336]

Figure 71
The Reading Room, attached to Ivy House, Nenthead.
[DP154341]

The cottages built by the Company for the smelters are very good; they are pleasantly situated on one side of the valley with a bank sloping to the Nent, laid out as gardens. The cottages have two large and high rooms, are properly drained and have a yard behind, with a coal cellar, dustbin, and privy. The only objection is that the rooms are only two in number, and this, for large families, is too few, and was complained of by some of the residents.[43]

This was mild criticism indeed when compared to the opprobrium that Dr Peacock heaped upon the houses built by miners, smelters and others elsewhere in Nenthead on land leased from the company. These Peacock described as 'defective, and some of them objectionable', and he further wrote:

There were never more than two rooms, sometimes very small and low. Some still had thatched roofs, without proper ceiling for the upper rooms. Sometimes there were no privies.[44]

No houses fitting this precise description survive in Nenthead today; it is likely that they were abandoned as the population of the area diminished, were swept away in later phases of rebuilding, or were remodelled in such a way that they are no longer discernible. The history of those houses not developed corporately by the London Lead Company is more difficult to ascertain, but it is likely that the legacy of company housing was a stimulus to the improvement of conditions nearby.

The planned centre of Nenthead offered much more than improved domestic accommodation. The Company built a Reading Room for the edification of its employees in 1833, a facility that proved sufficiently popular to merit rebuilding in 1855 and enlargement in 1859 (Fig 71). This small and unassuming single-storey building, built as an annex to Ivy House, has been claimed as England's first free public library. Not only was it a particularly enlightened form of provision some 17 years before the national Public Libraries Act began the gradual trend towards municipally funded free library services, it was also central to the ethos of the company village, offering competition for the bawdier attractions of the nearby Miners Arms public house. Drinking alcohol, which was not compatible with Quaker beliefs and contributed to poverty and social disorder, was discouraged (Fig 72); by 1842 the London Lead Company's penalty for drunkenness was instant dismissal.[45]

Figure 72
A drawing entitled 'Fighting; effects of Alston Brewery …', below right. The scene takes place outside a building that bears a striking resemblance to the former Horse and Waggon in Nentsberry, below (© Science Museum/Science & Society Picture Library).
[DP143586]

In addition to this concern with the intellectual nourishment of its employees, the London Lead Company provided for the elementary education of their children. A non-denominational school had been set up by the company as early as 1818, and from a modest start within the company offices, it moved later to a small purpose-built structure, then expanded further in the 1860s. A new Nenthead School was completed in 1864 on a prominent position overlooking the centre of the village at the end of Church Lane, making a significant impact on this important site, with its symmetrical Gothic elevations and a characteristically steep roof pitch (Fig 73).

There was a degree of further residential development in Nenthead and Garrigill during the course of the 19th century, the area where most lead-mining activity took place. In Nenthead, speculative housing was developed in the Holmsfoot area along the Alston road, which lacked the standards and planned approach of the London Lead Company's corporate development of

Figure 73
Nenthead School, now the village hall.
[DP154348]

Figure 74
Cottages with banded rubble masonry on the west side
of the Green, Garrigill.
[DP154238]

Hillersdon Terrace. New housing developments in Garrigill were of a similar pedigree to those in Holmsfoot. Here, it was usual to employ local vernacular materials in the scattered examples of row or semi-detached housing seen around the Green from the mid- to late 19th century; the rubble walls were often decorated with bands of contrasting colours, as seen on Tynedale House and Bridge View (Fig 74). The overall design ambition of this mid-century housing tended to be lower than that of the corporately conceived dwellings built earlier.

Nenthead made a strong impression on 19th-century visitors, who encountered a modern industrial village surrounded by all the detritus of mineral extraction and processing. Walter White wrote in 1859 of his visit to the area during a holiday in the north of England:

> four miles from Alston, [we] come to the village of Nent Head, which makes no secret of its vocation, for huge mounds of refuse, tramways, wagons, heaps of ore, implements scattered about, and a sturdy population proclaim that it lives by the mines.[46]

White also wrote, 'Is it not right that a village should harmonise with its environment?' Thus the spoil heaps surrounding the buildings of Nenthead and Overwater remain an important part of Nenthead's historic character today, as visible remains of the legacy of the London Lead Company.

The reconstruction of churches and chapels

A significant architectural legacy of this period in Alston Moor was created by the various religious denominations which ministered to the inhabitants. There was considerable expansion in the religious life of the area, primarily emanating from the Methodist movement but also from the Church of England. Nonconformist chapels intended to serve the smaller settlements were also built during this period and there was a continual expansion of capacity overall, with new places of worship later rebuilt and extended. These buildings were, in part, a belated response to the significant population increases experienced within the parish in the late 18th and early 19th centuries, as well as a reflection of the growing enthusiasm for religious observance during the period.

The rise in the population of Alston Moor was mirrored in the new Christian denominations which attracted many of the miners and agricultural workers. The two reconstructions of St Augustine's were tacit attempts by the Church of England to win back worshippers who had flocked to the well-established Quaker, Dissenting and Methodist congregations from as early as the 17th century. These denominations offered a more egalitarian form of Christianity particularly attractive to those who lived and worked in harsh, poverty-ridden conditions. Many Methodist chapels were built in the parish from the 1760s onwards; this is an early date for the permanent construction of chapels at a time when most communities met in houses but is comparable to those for other mining areas, particularly in Cornwall. Few of these early chapels survive – most of the area's examples date from the later 19th century.

So, because of the poor state of its fabric and the competition from rival denominations, St Augustine's was rebuilt in 1769–70 to a design by Smeaton, the engineer frequently employed by Greenwich Hospital in its work in Alston Moor. Its outline appears on Fryer and Hilton's map of 1775, showing that it was a rectangular preaching box dignified only by a small tower at its western extremity and by a polygonal east end. The effect was of plainness and simplicity, but it was not large enough, or grand enough, for a later generation and it was rebuilt for a second time. J W Walton's designs for the nave, south aisle and chancel were executed between 1869 and 1870, with a tower and spire designed by G D Oliver completed in the south-west corner in 1886. It is one of the largest buildings in Alston Moor, its spire dominating Alston's skyline and acting as a clear signifier of the historic core of the town (Fig 75).

The 18th-century population growth of Garrigill and its surrounding area was reflected in alterations to the church of St John. Around 1752 a gallery was added to expand the seating, but it proved insufficient and eventually the church was rebuilt entirely in 1790. The Church of England's mission was strengthened during this period by establishing first a chapel and then a new church in the fast-growing Nenthead. Land adjacent to Hillersdon Terrace was granted by the London Lead Company in 1843 and in August 1845 the new church of St John the Evangelist was consecrated. Designed by Ignatius Bonomi and John Augustus Cory, it is broadly Decorated Gothic in style and highly restrained in its plan and detailing, with an unaisled nave and unrendered rubble walls both inside and out. Bonomi, whose practice was based in

Figure 75
St Augustine's church, situated in the heart of Alston with its spire dominating the town.
[DP154146]

Durham, had been much employed by the London Lead Company, particularly in their work at Middleton in Teesdale.

However, the relative size and number of chapels built by the dissenting denominations was indicative of the competition faced by the Church of England, as slow to react to the need for more churches in the North Pennines as it had been elsewhere in upland and industrial areas of England. An elegant Congregational chapel was constructed at Redwing, just to the north of Garrigill, in 1752 to replace the dissenting chapel at Loaning Head, but by the end of the century it was Methodism that was attracting significant congregations. By the mid-19th century, surveys demonstrated the extent to which the mining population had turned almost exclusively to Methodism. It was successful not only because it provided more numerous and convenient places of worship, but also because of the more proselytising manner with which it addressed the spiritual needs of miners and their families. The original Wesleyan form of Methodism was increasingly challenged by Primitive Methodism, a more charis-matic version which grew quickly in popularity: surveys of religious attendance showed that between 1840 and 1851 Primitive Methodism overtook the Wesleyan form in terms of weekly attendance at services.[47]

Primitive Methodism naturally required its own community infrastructure and chapels, and the first of these to be constructed in Alston Moor was in Whitehall, an outlying area of Nenthead, in 1823. The site was redeveloped in 1847, when a schoolroom was added and the chapel itself rebuilt. In the Gatehead area of Garrigill, meanwhile, the Primitive Methodists were extremely prolific, building a chapel in 1825 and then successively rebuilding it to keep pace with expanding congregations – first in 1856 to accommodate 400 people and, as demonstrated by the date stone on the existing building, in another phase of development in 1885. In its final incarnation, the chapel displays many features typical of Methodist places of worship in general and Primitive Methodist chapels in particular, with the expression of overt style kept to a mini-mum and a close correspondence between form – essentially a rectangular preaching box – and function (Fig 76).

The Wesleyan Methodists enjoyed a similar building boom. The new model village settlement at Nenthead was furnished with a chapel as early as 1827; it is shown on the 1828 company plans and was remodelled in 1873 to create the imposing building seen today. In Alston, successive Wesleyan chapels were

Figure 76
The former Primitive Methodist chapel, Garrigill.
[DP143597]

abandoned in favour of a substantial new building in the expanding area of Townhead, realised in 1867–8 to designs by R F N Haswell of North Shields. This chapel represents the architectural tour de force of 19th-century Methodism in Alston Moor, its impressive massing relieved by a colourful combination of red and yellow sandstone (Fig 77). Built for 600 worshippers, it is by far the largest chapel in the parish and dominates many views in and of the town, representing a bold statement of the vitality of the congregation that built it.

Figure 77
St Paul's Methodist chapel, Townhead, Alston, formerly
Wesleyan and now redundant.
[DP154250]

Public and commercial buildings

Numerous schools were created in Alston Moor during the 19th century by a number of local organisations, before the introduction of the 1870 (Forster) Education Act brought about national educational reform. Although not all of them survive, there remains a considerable legacy of the step-change in educational provision that occurred in the mid-19th century. In Garrigill, a girls' school was first constructed in 1850 and extended in 1874, supported by landed and charitable endowment – particularly by Greenwich Hospital, which granted the original land for the building. Architecturally, the school differs substantially from other school buildings in the parish constructed during the same period, having a particularly domestic character with its two storeys, projecting porch and roughcast render. Now converted to residential use, there is little to indicate that it was once a school, save for a large red sandstone plaque set into the first floor of the main elevation.

Alston Grammar School was among the first institutions to benefit from the trend towards renewed educational provision in the parish, when it was rebuilt by public subscription in 1828 on the same site on the Townhead stretch of Front Street that it had occupied since at least the later 18th century. The building is a straightforward but high-quality single-storey structure; it is currently the town's fire station. A stone plaque over the central doorway commemorates the rebuilding of the school, a fee-paying institution that was also endowed by local landowners, particularly Greenwich Hospital which gave £10 per annum towards its running costs. The other major legacy of school building during this period is the Salvin Schools complex, situated between The Butts and Kings Arms Lane. Sponsored and managed by the hugely influential Hugh Salvin, vicar of the parish during this period, the first of these school buildings was constructed in 1844 under the terms of a scheme supported by the National Society for Promoting Religious Education. Immediately adjacent, a mixed elementary school for 100 children was erected in 1851, again under the direction of Salvin. A little more accomplished than its near neighbour, it has a stone bellcote rising above the southern gable (Fig 78).

If one were to judge by Alston's town hall, there was no shortage of self-confidence in the town in the middle of the 19th century (Fig 79). Constructed in 1857 to the exuberant design of A B Higham of Newcastle, it provided a

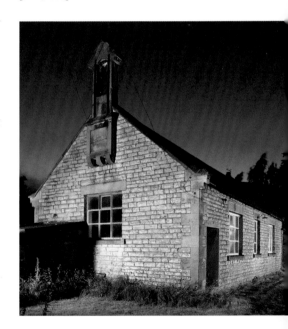

Figure 78
The second of the schools in Alston built under the auspices of the Revd Hugh Salvin.
[DP143601]

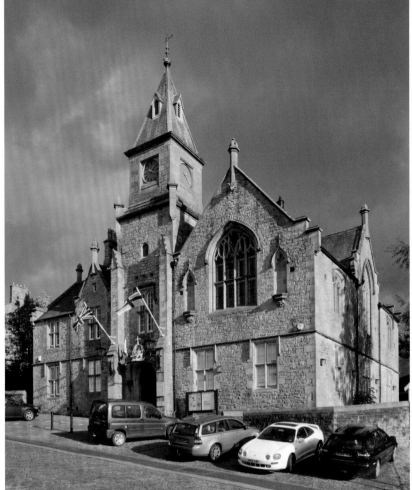

Figure 79 (right)
Alston Town Hall, decked out for the Queen's Diamond Jubilee.
[DP143602]

Figure 80 (below)
The monument at Townfoot to the mine owner Jacob Walton (1809–1863), who once lived at Greenends, north-west of Nenthead.
[DP155001]

range of functions for the town council and the community, including a reading and news room, a court room, a space for the local Literary Society and a large hall hosting events for up to 400 people. Its powerful design, broadly reminiscent of the 15th and 16th centuries, has an asymmetrical plan and a central clock tower; it dominates views of the lower town. Other components of civic life from the 19th century are similarly conspicuous in the townscape: the police station built in the late 1840s is architecturally unremarkable, but commands a key corner site in the Townhead area at the junction of the Nenthead and Garrigill roads, while an 1864 monument to local mining entrepreneur and dignitary Jacob Walton, an eye-catcher of Gothic and Classical forms, is constructed in various colours of granite and lends a rare tone of textural and chromatic diversity to Townfoot (Fig 80).

Front Street gained a number of new commercial premises without ever fully losing its character as an 18th-century high street with various vernacular features. While a small number of these premises, such as the current HSBC bank on the corner of the Market Place, date from the second half of the 19th century and represent a keener sense of commercial pomp than had been seen before, albeit executed in the materials and style of older buildings, it was more common for existing properties to be refronted in order to raise their status. Typically, it was a change in texture and stylistic execution that charac-terised these refrontings, with only a limited shift to modern or geographically distant materials such as the red and golden sandstone of Barclays Bank from 1898 (formerly the Carlisle and Cumberland Bank) and the Welsh slate seen on certain roofs once the arrival of the railway in 1852 made deviation from local materials a realistic possibility.

A landscape of agricultural improvement

When Thomas Pennant approached Alston Moor from Hartside in 1773, he experienced

> a most dreary view of a black tract, and some poor collieries: came to a narrow vale, cultivated on both sides, and watered by the Tyne, here an inconsiderable stream arising out of a fell a few miles to the south.[48]

Cultivation in the 18th century was evidently limited to the lower valley slopes, well below the remaining traces of medieval strip farming. In contrast, Hodgson noted in 1840 that more and more land higher up the slopes was being brought into use for better-quality grazing and hay cropping: constant land improvement was making Alston Moor's farmsteads more productive, and by this date animals grazed the fells for 9 months out of 12 (Fig 81). For Hodgson:

> wild and stormy as its mountain tops are … the sides of its largest streams are embroidered with meadows of the brightest green, and every succeeding autumn speckled with broader patches of cultivated ground.[49]

Figure 81
Improved fields with dry stone walls.
[DP154266]

Land improvement, especially in the late 18th and 19th centuries, usually took two forms: draining and liming. Water was the great adversary when it came to maintaining sweet pasture: it drowned the good grass and encouraged reeds and other rank vegetation. The answer, applied around Alston at least as early as the mid-18th century, was under-drainage, or 'soughing', which carried away water without impeding cultivation or other forms of soil improvement. The earliest examples, associated with long-established farms such as Whitlow and Annat Walls, consist of stone-built conduits or rubble-filled trenches, buried within or linked to natural drainage channels. Later systems, especially those associated with the reclamation of moors and commons in the early 19th century, tend towards more rigorous grid-like or 'herringbone' patterns and cover the fields with such intensity that one wonders if there might be as much stone laid beneath the ground as contained within the surrounding walls. In the final stages, however, stone was replaced by ready-made ceramic pipes delivered to Alston along the railway.

Further improvements were made by breaking the surface and spreading lime, the benefits of which (essentially the reduction in soil acidity) had been known, if not precisely understood, since the early 16th century. In the lower valley fields lime was simply applied to land which had long since been cleared and occasionally cultivated. Moorland, on the other hand, required more drastic steps – typically the burning and ploughing-in of existing vegetation – before it was worth introducing the lime and re-seeding. Lime was produced by the controlled burning of limestone in numerous field-kilns, examples of which can be found throughout the district, and in larger, more centralised concerns, such as Jackson's Limekilns at the foot of Bayle Hill. Draining and liming allowed farmers to increase their production of meat and milk substantially; it required considerable investment, but this was presumably exceeded by the profits to be made supplying the growing mining population in the 18th and early 19th centuries.

Agriculturally, Alston Moor continued to produce small quantities of cereals in the more favoured parts of the valleys while livestock was pastured on the hills above. Wheat prices fluctuated considerably during the period, affecting both producers and consumers and leading to periods of great hardship. Under such pressures, the enclosure of substantial areas of common grazing, and the parcelling out of the resulting fields to individual occupiers, was advocated as

Figure 82 (opposite)
A landscape of improvements above the South Tyne valley.
[DP154166]

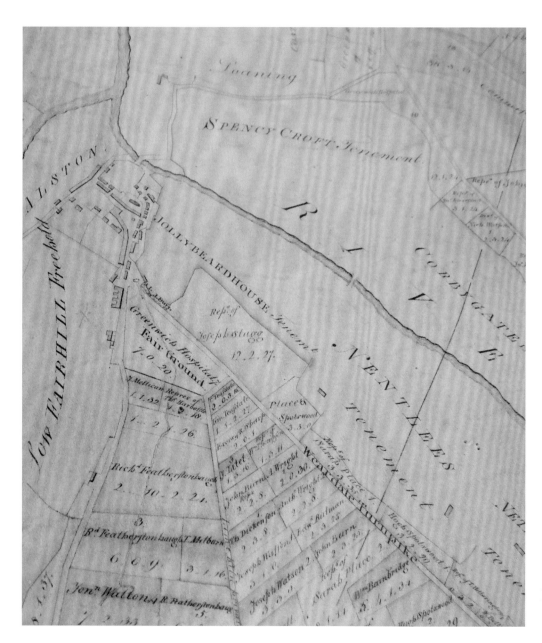

Figure 83
A detail of the area south of
Alston from the 1820 parish
Enclosure map.
[© CAS, ref. QRE 1/108]

a way of improving productivity. In Alston Moor the process started with the Act of Enclosure of 1803, though it took until 1820 to be fully executed in the majority of Alston Moor, the final Act for the 'Inclosure of the Manor of Whitlaw' (Whitlow) coming in 1862. Ruler-straight boundaries marking these new fields are still a striking characteristic of the landscape around Alston: the walls marching relentlessly upwards, blind to the lie of the land, but perfectly aligned with the allotments drawn up by the surveyors (Fig 82). Pride in the acquisition of a new allotment is sometimes reflected in massive gateposts with ornate ironwork, found in some surprisingly remote locations high on the moors. 'Drifts' and 'occupation roads', some carefully engineered to allow the easy movement of carts, were constructed to allow controlled movement through a landscape in which access had hitherto been unimpeded. Some roads, indeed some small plots of land, were specifically to allow people to mine coal, quarry stone and carry out other activities to which they had rights on the former common land.

Rather than many new farmsteads being constructed, many existing farms extended their land further up the gradient, resulting in the development of larger linear farmsteads and more ranges of outbuildings; the surviving enclosure maps of 1820 show how much more of the high fells were brought into the hands of individual farmers (Fig 83). Rare new farmsteads of the post-enclosure period include Moscow Farm and Leipsic [Leipzig] Farm, located on newly enclosed land east of Clarghyll Hall, their names commemorating two decisive defeats of Napoleon in 1812 and 1813, respectively. This was just the beginning of radical change for the planning of farmsteads in Alston Moor. By the late 19th century, small to medium-sized farmsteads had developed into dispersed cluster plans with buildings seemingly randomly grouped together, formed into groups with one or two buildings set around a yard or linked together to form a regular L-plan. In most cases, however, these plans represent growth from an earlier linear range.

New farmhouses of the early 19th century were very simple in design, walled in thinly coursed rubble, with sash windows and shallow pitched roofs. Foul Loaning is an example of a rebuilt farmhouse of the period, while that at Ameshaugh was newly built. The latter is tacked onto the end of a linear run of earlier bastles, but has the sash windows, rubble walls, quoins and a rusticated doorway typical of the period (Fig 84). Others, such as The Rise near Nattrass

Figure 84 (left)
The new farmhouse at Ameshaugh, built onto one end of the earlier linear farmsteads. It is two-storeyed but has no byre or basement, a sign that Alston's buildings of the period were now in line with national norms. [DP155002]

Figure 85 (below)
The armorial plaque dated 1746, celebrating the renovation of Randalholme by the Richardson family. [BB99/02605]

Gill, were purpose-built as linear farmsteads, although with byres and barns to one side of the house instead of underneath. As Hodgson noted in 1840, farmhouses and cottages across Alston Moor were whitewashed during the early 19th century, as they may have been for centuries before. Traces of whitewash remain on many farmsteads, including Nettle Hall and Low Park; the technique not only made the buildings more visible in the landscape – vital in poor weather conditions – but also protected the rubble and lime-mortar walling from the elements.[50]

Smaller country seats

Away from Alston itself, some farmsteads were upgraded to form residences for the better-off portion of Alston Moor society, who were in some cases senior officials in the mining industry. The expansion of South Loaning House from farmstead to gentrified house was carried out for a mine agent by the name of Dickenson in the middle of the 18th century. By 1829, it was the home of Thomas Sopwith, another mine agent and author of one of the first books about Alston Moor. At Randalholme, the tower house was improved with the insertion of sash windows and the removal of its parapet; the armorial carving on its north elevation, dated 1746 and inscribed with the initials 'C.R.R.', for Christopher Randal Richardson (Fig 85), may mark the completion of this work. At Low Lovelady Shield, the old tenement was transformed by the

Figure 86 (right)
Low Lovelady Shield.
[DP154188]

Figure 87 (below)
The Italianate entrance tower to Nent Hall, proudly displaying the lion rampant and a Latin motto frequently used by members of the Wilson family; this translate as 'Always vigilant'.
[DP155003]

Dickinson family (solicitors) with the construction of a handsome, late 18th-century house (Fig 86). Harbut Lodge, meanwhile, overlooking the South Tyne valley, is one of the parish's largest and most architecturally accomplished houses. Dating from 1838 and built for Hugh Friend, it is broadly classical in both plan and detailing and includes such refined features as ashlar masonry. Along with Alston House, it is an isolated example of the use of ashlar in the parish. Later industrialists continued to transform farmsteads into grander houses. The Wilson family, who included Thomas, a director of the Newcastle and Carlisle Railway, remodelled the farmstead of Nent Hall in 1858 into a vision of Italianate Cumberland (Fig 87); it was grand enough to be occupied in 1901 by Auguste Malherbe – the chief accountant to Vieille Montagne, the successors of the London Lead Company in Nenthead – and his family.

The extensive physical change across Alston during the 18th and 19th centuries is the most significant legacy of the lead industry in its prime. While the scars of mineral extraction in the landscape are faded but still visible, the houses and public buildings of the period, while not immediately revealing a great deal of their provenance, remain a monument to the flow of people, money and confidence through the area at a time when lead mining was still considered to be part of the future.

4

Decline and diversification, 1882–1949

In the latter decades of the 19th century, Alston Moor experienced a catastrophic deterioration of its industrial base with the collapse of its centuries-old lead industry. Hopes that the mining of zinc would restore its fortunes quickly evaporated and, as the 20th century progressed, the area seemed destined to revert to a pastoral monoculture. Where the early 19th century had been characterised by intense pressure on the building stock, leading to subdivision and overcrowding in many instances, the late 19th and early 20th centuries saw massive depopulation and the abandonment of countless houses and mine buildings (Fig 88). As more accessible parts of rural England were colonised by commuters and second-home owners, Alston Moor languished. Such conditions have a devastating impact on some aspects of the historic environment, but they spare others.

The end of mining and its effects

The long-term deterioration of the local economy from the 1830s was masked for some years, but had become inexorable by the end of the 19th century. The primary factor driving this collapse was the fluctuating price of lead on the world market, but it was also affected by the ability of other regions, particularly Canada, to surpass areas like Alston in terms of natural reserves and industrial efficiency. The defining crisis came during the 1870s when a crash in the global price of lead meant that the London Lead Company – easily the single largest mining concern in Alston Moor – found it uneconomic to continue their operation, resulting in their departure in 1882.

The importance of the London Lead Company to Alston Moor cannot be exaggerated. The company had been the driving force behind the development of the parish from a largely agricultural economy to one dominated by lead mining, had developed Nenthead and Garrigill from small farming settlements into the substantial villages they are today and had provided a framework, alongside Greenwich Hospital as lords of the manor, within which much of the population operated for 200 years. This was the point at which the modern history of Nenthead and Alston Moor altered irrevocably as the corporate paternalism that had guided architectural patronage and the wider cultural life of the area for two centuries was abruptly wound up. While the economy was

Figure 88
Industrial change in Nenthead encapsulates many of the trends of economic decline and transition across Alston Moor.
[DP154323]

by no means closed down by this action, all the confidence that had under-pinned the previous investment in cultural and religious institutions quickly drained away.

Subsequent holders of extraction leases from the Greenwich Hospital Estate – initially the Nenthead and Tynedale Lead and Zinc Company from 1882, the Belgian-owned Vieille Montagne Zinc Company from 1896 and finally Anglo-Austral Mines Ltd from 1949 – diversified into minerals other than lead, notably zinc and later fluorspar, but even these vestigial operations were uneconomical by the 1950s. The Vieille Montagne Zinc Company brought an international tone to the parish, though its integrated operations reduced the overall numbers of workers required in mining processes. The smelting of the zinc ore, for instance, now took place in the company's home in Belgium; dressed ore was transported by road to Alston station and thence by train and ship to the European mainland.[51] The shift away from both the traditional methods of the mineral extraction industry and the established social structures of the local population was symbolised by the construction in Nenthead of a large new ore-dressing plant, also known as the gravity mill, in 1908 (Figs 88 and 89). This building, designed on a substantial scale and utilising the still-novel constructional technology of steel framing with brick infill panels, was a clear expression of the mechanised and increasingly internationalised industry that mineral extraction had become by the early 20th century. Its construction required Vieille Montagne to clear much of the 19th-century heart of Nenthead, demolishing the market hall, clock tower and public baths. While it harmed the architectural integrity of the 19th-century village created by the London Lead Company, it nevertheless expressed confidence in the continuing viability of the mining industry and a need for new investment and technology.[52] A more mechanised approach was replacing the labour-intensive, labour-welfare systems of the 19th century.

The effect of the First World War was to reduce the number of men of mining age in the parish, setting off a chain of events that resulted in the closure of some levels in 1918 and the final withdrawal of Vieille Montagne from the Nenthead mines in 1921.[53] Although the company continued to operate locally until the 1940s in three smaller locations at Brownley Hill, Nentsberry and Rotherhope, mineral extraction in Alston Moor was gradually coming to an end. A number of different industries, mainly other forms of mineral or aggregate

Figure 89
Nenthead Gravity Mill, built by the Vieille Montagne
Zinc Company, shown in its original state soon
after construction.
[© Carlisle Library, Cumbria County Council]

extraction (Fig 90), were either continued or established during the inter-war period, but this was undoubtedly a time of severe economic hardship and consequent migration in search of jobs. One noted scheme to try to relieve unemployment during this difficult period was instigated by the Revd Norman Walton, who began operating the Alston Lime and Coal Company out of North Loaning and Blagill, employing two dozen men.[54] In 1949, the Vieille Montagne Zinc Company pulled out of Alston Moor completely, selling their mineral extraction leases to Anglo-Austral Mines Ltd, a mining concern that switched attention away from lead and zinc altogether and firmly towards fluorspar extraction.[55]

During the Second World War, an unexpected new strand in the economy of Alston Moor was established as a direct result of the wartime government policy of favouring inland locations for munitions manufacturing. A new steel foundry producing mortar-bomb cases was established next to a former woollen mill on the banks of the Nent in Alston. The Alston Foundry was originally an offshoot of Steel Co Ltd based in Sunderland, but passed through various owners and prospered in peacetime as much as in wartime, moving on to manufacture mining equipment for the nationalised coal industry after the war.[56] Further manufacturing took place on the old Alston Brewery site on the River South Tyne which, by 1906, had become a hosiery factory.[57]

Figure 90
Coal mining is still carried out today in Alston Moor, at a site near Clargill.
[DP154244]

Development in the farmsteads

As the economic powerhouse of the lead industry declined dramatically, effecting steep population decline in the main settlements, farming again became Alston Moor's principal employer. Subsequently, improvements were carried out at many of the farmsteads in the late 19th and early 20th century, but in some cases this pattern of development led to the change of use, and sometimes the abandonment, of their vernacular buildings. Low Park, a farm to the north of Alston in the South Tyne valley, offers a typical example: a substantial new detached farmhouse of a conservative design was constructed in the mid- to late 1920s to stand in the garden of a linear range of 17th- and 18th-century buildings which had previously provided every farmstead function under one roof (Fig 91). The core of this range was a bastle, which appears to have been occupied until the new house was built. By the 20th century, if not before, domestic accommodation placed over a byre was likely to be considered unfit for human habitation. Once downgraded from domestic to agricultural use, the vernacular buildings of Low Park were used intensively and adapted, with a noticeable impact on their fabric. The bastle portion of the old linear farmstead had its floor removed in order to operate more effectively as a hay barn and the northern portion of the range was demolished and replaced with a modern milking shed in the 1950s.

This pattern of agricultural conversion was repeated throughout the parish. At the complex, linear sequence of bastles at Annat Walls, for instance, the southern end was given over entirely to storage, with many of the floors and some partitions removed, while the one family remaining in what was once a multi-occupancy site retreated to the dedicated domestic accommodation at the northern end. At one time, Ameshaugh's linear bastle farmstead had extensive domestic use, but once the new farmhouse was built onto the linear range in the middle of the 19th century it became used as animal sheds, barns and storage. In some ways, this evolving use of historically important buildings as their status declined has been detrimental to their condition and their fabric has been substantially altered. However, in other ways it has had the effect of preserving structures that might otherwise have been abandoned to dereliction. Though the history of old bastle ranges on farmsteads can be quite complex to interpret, that they have survived at all is due to their continuing usefulness to

farming families, providing well-built and adaptable accommodation whether domestic or agricultural.

A handful of farmsteads were completely rebuilt in the late 19th century, reflecting an unusual degree of investment in agriculture in Alston Moor at this time. These regular, planned farmsteads are rare in the parish, and are on a smaller scale than those in lowland areas. Low Crossgill in the Tynehead area south of Garrigill and Wanwood Hill in the South Tyne valley offer examples of farms that gained particularly architecturally refined farmhouses towards the end of the 19th century, indicative of a small tier of agricultural wealth that created something more akin to small, prosperous estates than prosaic family farmsteads. Wanwood Hill, for instance, was transformed into a regular planned farmstead arranged around a courtyard, with a farmhouse positioned on its southern side. A datestone of 1746 has been reset in one of the agricultural ranges, but most of the building dates from the end of the 19th century.

Figure 91
Low Park, with its linear bastle range and a new farmhouse of the 1920s.
[DP109734]

Shooting lodges

This level of polite domestic architecture in scattered rural locations has often become integrated into the ever-popular market for grouse shooting, providing suitably grand accommodation for visiting shoots. The double-fronted farmhouse at Low Crossgill (Fig 92) now functions as a shooting lodge, for instance, but there has been a trend for converting farm buildings in this way for quite some time. Rotherhope Tower is an old linear farmstead, probably of a similar antiquity to comparable sites elsewhere; it was given a castellated, Gothic treatment in the late 19th century to cater for shooting parties who must have come for the romance of the wild border region as much as for the quality of the game. Wanwood, the farmstead next to Wanwood Hill, was nearly tripled in size by the addition of a large block for domestic accommodation in the late

Figure 92
Low Crossgill acquired a new farmhouse in 1877
and some of the old linear farmstead was subsequently
demolished, leaving a roof scar of a structure that
was once thatched with heather.
[DP154210]

Figure 93
Wanwood combines an old linear farmstead with
extensive accommodation, creating a prime late 19th-
century shooting lodge.
[DP154231]

19th century (Fig 93). With its massive, angled chimney stack and mullioned windows, it fits admirably with an Arts and Crafts aesthetic. In 1906 it was the residence and shooting lodge of William Peers King, a man of considerable means who may have been responsible for its construction.[58] At this date, King also employed a gamekeeper who lived on the premises.

Indeed, the reputation – and exclusivity – of Alston's shooting has an even longer pedigree. As early as 1825, the topographical writer Eneas Mackenzie was able to state that the area 'affords excellent grouse-shooting; but the manors are so strictly preserved, that the miners are deprived of their favourite amusements of hunting and shooting on their dreary moors'.[59] The Commissioners of Greenwich Hospital were keen to acquire more land in Alston Moor in the first half of the 20th century in order to protect their game interests. They purchased Ivy House in Garrigill in 1929 and Gatehead Farm, Garrigill, in 1934 because they were worried that their 'acquisition by a netter or for that matter any other party might seriously affect the Crossgill Shooting'.[60] Netting was a practice of erecting nets in which to catch the grouse, enabling the netter to profit at the expense of the sportsman. Today, the large shooting estates cater for the considerable demand for the area's rare black grouse, however little integrated into the local economy and the lives of the majority of local people this is. Though the architectural impact of country pursuits remains slight and somewhat disguised, the interconnectedness of shooting, agriculture and land management generally is of considerable economic significance for Alston Moor. This has been the case for quite some time, and game rights have formed an acutely important aspect of many property sales over the decades.

Civic infrastructure

Little housing was erected in the inter-war period, with the exception of the Raise, which saw the construction of a small lane of bungalows at Raise Hamlet and a few pairs of houses (Fig 94). Instead, the principal building projects were mostly of a municipal nature. Educational institutions in the area were increasingly shaped by national legislation and local authority funding and provision. The primary school in Nenthead, for instance, funded formerly by the Greenwich Hospital and the London Lead Company, was re-established as a Board School in 1899 under the control of Cumberland County Council and

Figure 94
Arts and Crafts-style bungalows at Raise Hamlet.
[DP143598]

relocated to a larger building in the Holmsfoot area of the village. Samuel King's School, meanwhile, constructed on the Garrigill Road in Alston in 1909, was part of the first generation of schools created under the terms of the 1902 (Balfour) Education Act. One of the earliest monuments to public welfare provision, in the period when Alston Moor left behind its history as a corporately controlled parish, the building freely and confidently uses numerous Edwardian design motifs, incorporating neo-Baroque, Queen Anne and Arts and Crafts features into its masonry structure (Fig 95).

The Ruth Lancaster James Cottage Hospital, completed in 1908 in the Townfoot area of Alston, was part of a gradual spread of such facilities nationally, although a relatively late arrival in a movement that first developed in the 1860s. Stylistically and in its plan, it is typical of its type, offering a small number of beds arranged in single-storey wards off a two-storey, mixed-use block; the design by T T Scott is worked in a broadly traditional idiom with

Figure 95
The Samuel King School, now the County Primary School, Alston.
[DP143600]

Figure 96
The Ruth Lancaster James Hospital.
[DP143599]

steeply pitched gables, displaying domestic detailing, textures and proportion (Fig 96). Alston was an obvious location for a cottage hospital, being very isolated from the nearest general hospital, and, aside from general community health needs, there were the additional concerns of industrial accidents requiring immediate treatment.

By the mid-20th century, the vital economic life of Alston Moor had declined to a point where just over 1,000 people were able to subsist in an area that provided only challenging agricultural land and a small manufacturing base to supplement a rural service sector. Nevertheless, there remained a rich architectural legacy, particularly of the achievements of the 17th, 18th and 19th centuries. The adaptation of existing buildings was both prudent and cost-effective at a time of excess provision due to population decline and changing expectations in both the agricultural and domestic spheres. This has created the scenario where a rather high proportion of vernacular buildings have survived, often recast into slightly different guises; they now form part of a special architectural legacy that is beginning to be better appreciated. The period after 1882 and the withdrawal of the London Lead Company was, then, one of consolidation, in economic, cultural and architectural terms. To a considerable degree the area had reached its fullest built extent; the most significant trends of the following decades though the First World War and up to the Second World War were those of an economy adjusting to new realities, a wider culture facing up to steep population decline and a hugely reduced impetus to build.

5

Regeneration and conservation, 1950 to the present

With the almost complete cessation of mining activity in Alston Moor, the area's post-war development followed patterns familiar to other upland areas of England, with a generally low rate of new building and a less locally distinctive tone in such work as did take place. A decline in traditional industries has been partially offset by the growth in tourism, but overall the impact of decreasing population and economic hardship has created a particular set of conservation challenges, especially for the area's vernacular buildings (Fig 97). The relative lack of dynamism in the economy has meant that development pressures were low (by national standards) in the second half of the 20th century and will continue to be so into the foreseeable future. The development that has taken place has focused largely on regenerating the existing stock of buildings. Where these have been designated assets (scheduled monuments, listed buildings and buildings in conservation areas), controls have developed over the last half-century to ensure that appropriate conservation standards are observed. Beyond the realm of statutory controls, perhaps the greatest impact on conservation can be attributed to the influence of local groups and individuals who are actively engaged with the promotion of Alston Moor's special historic character.

Probably the greatest threat to this character is that the growth in new industries such as tourism, and the positive impact made by new residents drawn to the natural beauty of the area and its other attractions, may not be sufficient to drive up demand for the high-quality conservation of existing buildings. This may make these buildings increasingly vulnerable to redundancy and dereliction. However, the uniqueness of Alston's historic environment is locally valued as a key component of its cultural and economic viability in the future, but there are many challenges to meet if the future of the historic environment itself is to be assured.

Post-war development in Alston Moor

Following the Second World War, much of the building that occurred across Alston Moor followed the familiar patterns of public and private development seen in schemes across the country. Building of any kind was not particularly extensive, however, as most forms of traditional economic stimulus withered

Figure 97
The historic building stock of Alston Moor provides many challenges and opportunities for the future.
[DP154180]

Figure 98
Aerial photograph showing the southern development
of Alston, with Church Road and the new Samuel
King's School.
[20682/024]

away and the historic character of most of the key settlements, and especially that of the rural hinterland, was extensively preserved. There were one or two examples of development in the second half of the 20th century that bucked this trend, creating complete landscapes that were the product of their era, with little sense of historic influence. At Church Road near the centre of Alston, a wholly late 20th-century portion of townscape was created in the 1950s with a scheme of municipal housing arranged in pairs and the creation of a new building for Samuel King's School (Fig 98). The school itself is of a fairly standard design for the period, though a good example and well maintained – its plate glass and coloured panel-clad steel frame is entirely expressive of a postwar welfare state architecture that strove for universal provision of services in an explicitly modern fashion. The two-storey council houses set an architectural tone which mixed a functional approach with a vernacular-inflected take on contemporary design trends, seen in the rubble-walled entrance canopies with their wave-shaped roofs. Though Church Road is just a few minutes' walk from the market cross and the centre of Alston, its built environment gives no hint of the wider historical context and conjures the sense of a discrete zone of development. The product of post-war systems of welfare and central government funding that affected the shape and appearance of many British towns, Church Road can be viewed as a modern successor to the model village scheme of Hillersdon Terrace and the tradition of corporate philanthropy from which it emerged.

Smaller municipal housing schemes were executed by the Alston and Garrigill District Council, such as Bevan Terrace and Vicarage Terrace in Overwater and Nenthead from the 1950s and 1960s respectively (Fig 99). These were the result of selective slum clearance around the parish and the requirement to provide improved housing standards, rather than an expansion of housing stock. A small amount of slum clearance took place in the heart of Alston at the Potato Market, which slightly reduced the density of the area and opened up some space now used for shoppers' parking, but this did not

Figure 99
Bevan Terrace, a small row of 1950s semi-detached housing, was constructed on the hill above Overwater, near Nenthead.
[DP154320]

Figure 100
Buildings around the Potato Market, south of the market place in Alston; these were cleared as part of the mid-20th-century slum clearance programme. [© Carlisle Library, Cumbria County Council]

particularly compromise the overall historic integrity of the centre (Fig 100). During the last quarter of the 20th century some more significant expansion took place outwards from Alston's historic core, with a few private residential estates such as The Firs and Bruntley Meadows and the expansion of The Raise at Middle Park, but only the formation of new households was able to stimulate this demand as there was no net population growth during the period. Far more significant than newly built private housing schemes like these was the general trend towards refurbishment of existing building stock as the social and economic structure of the area began to shift towards the end of the 20th century.

Regeneration

As property prices in the area became increasingly competitive compared to those in neighbouring areas of highly desirable countryside such as the Yorkshire Dales and the Lake District from the 1970s onwards, Alston Moor attracted newcomers keen to take up a rural lifestyle. This gradual shift in the population has had telling effects and moved the area through a process of partial gentrification, particularly noticeable in a few hotspots. More concerted redevelopment has focused on Alston's town centre. The Butts, in particular, has seen significant investment. This is one of the oldest residential areas of the town centre, with a high density of domestic accommodation arranged mostly in rows, largely pre-dating 1800 and clustered around a network of narrow lanes, some of which were subject to a slum clearance order in 1930. The Alston Art Apartments, one of the most recent of the restoration schemes from 2008, created a sequence of renovated cottages, some for holiday lets and some for permanent occupation, largely from extant buildings (Fig 101). The Butts is full of historically sensitive sites, typical of the character of Alston's vernacular buildings, and the project has preserved much of the fabric of the older buildings, in combination with some new rubble walling, slate roofs and wooden balconies looking onto the churchyard of St Augustine's church. Indeed, some of the most distinctive features of Alston's vernacular traditions such as upstairs living have been preserved in a number of the restored cottages in The Butts and elsewhere, and their use of traditional rubble walling for both restored and new portions helps them blend well with the surrounding environment. The

Figure 101
Alston Art Apartments, part of a heritage-led development in The Butts, Alston.
[DP154224]

Alston Art Apartments won the New Build category of Eden District Council's 2009 Design Awards.

Although the mining legacy of the area is visible across much of the landscape in numerous earthworks, the majority of the built environment does not explicitly reveal this history. The founding of the North Pennines Heritage Trust in 1987 and the subsequent development of the Nenthead Mines Heritage Centre quickly became the focus of a tourist industry that embraced the area's industrial past, preserving the key structures and mining levels at Nenthead as a tourist attraction and acting as a resource for archaeologists, other researchers and anyone with a general interest in discovering more of the region's rich legacy of mineral extraction (Fig 102). The development of tourism as a key part of the area's economy has not only helped to preserve these physical monuments to the industrial past, but has also supported the conservation of various structures housing the galleries, shops and cafes that have developed alongside the core visitor attractions. Sadly, Nenthead Mines Heritage Trust and Centre have recently gone into administration, although at the time of writing the newly formed Nenthead Mines Conservation Society is seeking a sustainable way forward for the site.

The natural beauty of the area (Fig 103) has also helped to stimulate the flow of visitors and money into Alston Moor: the designation of the North

Figure 102
The Barracks at Nenthead Mines.
[DP154310]

Figure 103 (opposite)
The natural beauty and challenges of Alston Moor's historic environment.
[DP154355]

Pennines as an Area of Outstanding Natural Beauty in 1988 was followed by accreditation first as a European Geopark in 2003 and a year later as a UNESCO Geopark in recognition of the international significance of the area's geology and other natural attributes. This status has helped to cement Alston Moor's reputation as an attractive place in which to stay, explore and engage in various outdoor activities, not least cycling. Alston, Garrigill and Nenthead have all benefited from their location along the Sea to Sea (C2C) National Cycle Route across the north of England, officially opened in 1994. At the luxury end of the tourist industry, shooting (particularly of black grouse) has grown significantly as a leisure activity in recent decades, building on its popularity from the 19th century onwards and in turn boosting the viability of the quality hotel market in the area.

The overall economic decline across Alston Moor has created challenges and opportunities in conservation, and these issues are playing out in key individual sites across the area. Some building types, such as Nonconformist chapels, are particularly threatened. The Methodists now share a home with the Catholic community at St Wulfstan's church in Alston and all of the purpose-built Methodist chapels are now redundant, being too numerous and large for current needs. Some are being considered for redevelopment. Nonconformist chapels contain key internal features, such as galleries with intricate iron balustrades and wooden seating, as well as large windows with stained glass, and any reuse or redevelopment needs to take account of them. Generally, they have been converted to residential use, as at the former Primitive Methodist chapel at Whitehall, above Nenthead, and the former Congregational chapel at Loaning Head, while the earliest surviving Methodist chapel in Alston along Back o' the Burn was converted into two houses in the early 19th century.

Two of Alston's chapels were redeveloped in the 1970s in quite different ways. The former Primitive Methodist chapel in Nenthead Road was split in half to create two houses, its windows replaced and its elaborate roof trusses hidden from view. A different approach can be found in the changes made to the former Independent (or Congregational) chapel: part exhibition space, part residential, it was the Gossipgate Gallery for many years. It preserves something of the spirit of the chapel in its redesign, echoing the concept of the galleries and staircases it once had and preserving some of its iron columns and stained glass windows. Now, the parish has four Methodist chapels standing

Figure 104
The Congregational chapel at Redwing, now redundant.
[DP071469]

empty – some on very prominent sites – including the important and elegant former Congregational chapel at Redwing; their sensitive and appropriate conversion will be an important challenge for the future (Fig 104).

The distinctiveness of Alston Moor

Many aspects of Alston Moor's historic environment are highly distinctive or even unique to the area and require closer understanding if they are to be appreciated fully and, where appropriate, protected effectively. There has been some acknowledgement of this in the designation of historic buildings, areas and archaeological remains, but a more developed sense of significance is needed if the wider heritage of the area is to be managed successfully for the benefit of future generations.

Archaeologically, the area contains an exceptional collection of prehistoric settlement sites and the trackways which connect them, surviving as earthworks as the result of the relatively benign management regime provided by pasture. The low level of arable culture and the concentration on sheep and cattle grazing have created conditions in which sites which have completely disappeared from the archaeological record elsewhere in England have lain undisturbed here for millennia. Only where major programmes of pasture improvement were carried out from the later 18th century, and where large-scale mining was concentrated, does this landscape not survive as an underlay to the modern one. A lack of archaeological survey work, before the present project, has prevented the appreciation of the true importance of this remarkable, detailed and fragile landscape. It remains highly susceptible to damage from agricultural improvement, from vehicles and from over-grazing, yet much still survives.

Over the course of history Alston Moor has been shaped by environmental and human factors that have given rise to a number of characteristic and even

Figure 105
Alston in the mist.
[DP154164]

exceptional building types and settlement patterns (Fig 105). The architectural history of the area clearly reflects the impact that a range of specialised economic activities, particularly pastoral farming and mining, have had on the lives of the people who have settled here over the centuries, in one of the highest and most isolated settled districts of England. Patterns of independent land ownership, coupled with the harsh environmental conditions of the North Pennine uplands, gave rise to specific agricultural practices and characteristically dispersed settlement. There is abundant evidence from the 17th to 19th centuries of the sometimes precarious living to be made from this inhospitable area, of progressive pacification and of the periodic booms linked to lead mining. The various strands of the mineral extraction industry made a crucial contribution to the upland economy and in turn influenced patterns of settlement, especially during the 18th and 19th centuries when the influence of large mining concerns such as the London Lead Company led to the creation of new nucleated settlements in the parish beyond the historic township of Alston.

The bastle building type, derived largely from the 16th-century border tradition of defensive farmhouses, is a highly distinctive feature of Alston Moor. Examples survive as single farmsteads and in a number of hamlets, and others undoubtedly remain to be identified. None of the examples within the parish can be convincingly traced to a pre-1600 defensible purpose; instead, they represent a continuation, in a period when cross-border hostilities had ceased or had diminished sharply, of a practice originally adopted with defensive intent (Fig 106). The ruined complex near Annat Walls contains a strikingly late example of this building form – dated 1707 – suggesting that long after endemic violence had subsided, the bastle tradition was adhered to either from custom or because it offered valued practical advantages. Indeed, the building type continued to develop throughout the 18th century, into what one might call the bastle derivative or house-over-byre: a building maintaining a ground-floor byre with a two-storey house above and a permanent exterior stair to its first-floor doorway. Middle Park is an example of this: its thin walls, large windows and long outshot on the uphill side make it very far from defensible, but the concept of a ground-floor byre with a house above it endures (see Fig 31).

Alston itself is doubly significant as a town of probably ancient origins that retains a very high proportion of its 17th- to 19th-century building stock.

The numerous distinctive features of the town's layout, including the narrow lanes and crooked alleys clustered around the principal street and market place, hold clues to its remote origins and illustrate, with the density of buildings lining these routes, the impact of rising population as the lead industry boomed. The town has a large number of buildings that constitute an urban variant of the bastle, with an external staircase up to a first-floor entrance and a ground floor offering separate accommodation, which may in different locations and at different periods have served as a shop, workshop, byre or tenement (Fig 107). Fryer and Hilton's 1775 map suggests just how prevalent

Figure 106
Low Park, near Raise. A good example of the development of the bastle from the first half of the 17th century. [DP109693].

Figure 107 (above)
An external stair in the Market Place, Alston, from c 1950.
[AA081235]

Figure 108 (below)
The fountain, Nenthead.
[DP154346]

the arrangement once was, but even today many first-floor entrances remain in use and others can be identified from the presence of blocked doorways – features which add considerably to the distinctive character of Alston's street-scape. The dominant character of the town remains vernacular in scale and building traditions, and haphazard in plan and evolution, but there are isolated instances of civic, ecclesiastical and commercial grandeur dating from the 19th century in schemes like the town hall and the rebuilding of St Augustine's church. Some of the properties on Front Street and the Market Place were refronted in the 19th century, but in the lanes and alleys earlier characteristics typically predominate; only rarely is a sense of the essential integrity of the historic environment not pervasive.

Nenthead and Garrigill, meanwhile, provide an interesting contrast in their patterns of settlement. Both were subject to the corporate influence of the London Lead Company from the late 18th century, but it was Nenthead that was completely transformed from a tiny farming hamlet consisting of a few vernacular farmsteads into a centre for the lead industry. Nenthead is an early example of an industrial model village which was as much philanthropic as it was profit-driven in its rationale and where company employees and their families were provided with a range of educational, social and sanitary benefits (Fig 108). Although about half the Company's development of the village survives (in the form of Hillersdon Terrace, the former Wesleyan Methodist chapel, Ivy House and the former Reading Room), its integrity was destroyed in the early 20th century by Vieille Montagne, who swept away many of the social buildings in order to erect the gravity mill. However, the village is still deeply connected to its mining past; its wide views across the surrounding landscape visually connect it with spaces once used for transport and processing, and the brooding presence of the truncated gravity mill lies at its heart. Garrigill, on the other hand, had a significant existence long before the dominance of the lead industry as a centre, since the Middle Ages, for this particularly far-flung part of Alston Moor. The village has a more enclosed and surprisingly lowland character, looking inwards to its level green and sheltered by many mature trees. The industrial part of its existence is not immediately evident, but it is identifiable in the common characteristics of many of the cottages and institutional buildings, which together point to a period of rapid population growth in the first half of the 19th century.

Overall, the most distinctive and collectively significant buildings in the area are not high-status houses, churches or civic structures (though there are notable examples in each category), but instead those derived from the local vernacular tradition, in which the bastle and its derivatives hold a special place. Farmsteads of all dates, whether or not a bastle origin can be identified, are a conspicuous element of the built environment that helps to define the landscape character of Alston Moor. More than half the surviving farmsteads in the area are of linear or L-plan, with the house attached in-line to the working buildings. These farmsteads vary in scale from the very small (between 10 metres and 19 metres in length), which are concentrated around Garrigill, to substantial farmsteads over 40 metres in length which are more commonly found further west in Cumbria. In many cases a linear farmstead has been enlarged, with detached buildings forming a dispersed group or a small courtyard group, both of which are distinctive farmstead types in the area. The tradition of combining domestic and agricultural buildings into one structure is also reflected in ways rarely seen outside the North Pennines; for example, animal housing can be found within an outshot along the rear of the house. The larger regular planned farmstead groups that typically developed across England from the late 18th century are rare in the area and are usually relatively small in scale; they are associated with high-status houses or later phases of enclosure of moorland.[61]

Existing protection

The value and significance of Alston's historic environment has been recognised in a limited number of statutory designations. The National Heritage List for England, last revised in Alston Moor during 1983–4, identifies many of the area's key buildings, mostly domestic and ecclesiastical, primarily in Alston and with a handful in Garrigill and Nenthead, but has little coverage of industrial buildings and practically none of the outlying hamlets and farmsteads. Perhaps the best-covered single building type is the large house, as exemplified by Randalholme, Clarghyll Hall and Harbut Lodge, but a good deal of the area's important vernacular building stock has not, to date, been recognised by this national protection regime (Fig 109).

Figure 109
Clarghyll Hall, one of the designated Heritage Assets of Alston Moor.
[DP154163]

As a result of English Heritage's Monuments Protection Programme, most of the more significant sites of industrial archaeology in Alston Moor were scheduled as ancient monuments during the 1990s; in most cases, the designations were not restricted to the core processing buildings but included large areas of mining landscape, including spoil-heaps, leats, adits and isolated shafts, mine shops and related structures. Scheduling underlined the national importance of these sites and in several cases has acted as a spur to the development of programmes of consolidation, repair and presentation intended to encourage tourist visits to Alston Moor. The availability of money from the Heritage Lottery Fund, as well as from the European Union and bodies such as English Heritage, enabled the development of the Nenthead Mines Visitor Centre where, before closure, visitors could receive an introduction to the lead-mining heritage of the area, view the remains of the ore-processing plant, visit a range of restored and interpreted buildings and even enjoy an accompanied walk through a historic mine. Smaller grant-aided schemes have seen the repair and presentation of individual landscape features such as the bingsteads (storage bins for the collection of processed ore before transportation to the smelt mill) at Hudgill and one or two isolated mine shops. As this book goes to press, key structures at Whitesyke and Bentyfield are being repaired as part of a programme coordinated by the North Pennines AONB Partnership, with funding from the Heritage Lottery Fund and English Heritage.

Other forms of designation at a local level fill some of the gaps left by national systems. Eden District Council has created two Conservation Areas in Alston Moor, out of a total of 24 under its authority.[62] The first of these, covering the centre of Alston (including Front Street, Back o' the Burn, much of Townfoot and The Butts) was declared in 1976 and formed the earliest official recognition of the area's historic worth. A later designation in 2000 gave the centre of Garrigill (Fig 110) the same level of protection, with the usual focus on maintaining the special visual character of areas as a whole and close attention paid in the local planning process to replacement windows, doors, roofing materials, wall rendering and paint schemes.

The Eden Local Plan, devised in 1996, sets out to manage change across the natural and built environment in a fully rounded way, taking into account specific conservation areas but also acknowledging that planning policy must consider the total environment, including historic assets wherever they are located. In terms of the renovation of former dwellings in Alston Moor that have fallen into disrepair and require urgent conservation work, council policy is to emphasise the importance of using traditional materials and a minimum of external alteration, the better to retain historic character. A more locally specific policy within this framework acknowledges that the national code restricting the re-use of long-abandoned isolated dwellings is not appropriate

Figure 110
The Green, Garrigill.
[DP154361]

for Alston Moor, where such buildings form the basic building block of traditional scattered settlement patterns. Applications for renovations of this kind are nevertheless subject to close attention and stringency in applying the rules on materials and other considerations, as isolated farmsteads and other structures are particularly visible in the landscape as well as being historically sensitive (Fig 111).

Alston Moor's inclusion in the North Pennines AONB reflects the appeal of the underlying landscape and its powerful influence on the character of the built environment, especially its vernacular buildings. The AONB status, combined with the inscription of the North Pennines as a UNESCO Geopark, provides a great deal of prestige to the area as a whole and promotes its natural attractions to locals and tourists alike. Tourism – whether from walking and cycling or from a desire to explore the area's landscape, history, buildings, geology, flora and fauna – boosts the area's economy and contributes significantly to the appreciation of Alston Moor beyond its own borders.

Local organisations such as the Alston Moor Historical Society and Epiacum Heritage are embedded in local efforts to recognise and promote the area's special characteristics and sense of place and are well placed to argue how these may be sustained under the auspices of the local planning system. Interest in local history and the built environment is particularly strong, as indicated through recent publications by Alastair Robertson, Peter Wilkinson and others. There have also been local initiatives to investigate the buildings of Alston, such as that by the North Pennines Town Project Group which resulted in 'Alston: study of buildings' in 1999.

The challenges and opportunities of the future

In the context of an economy that has altered irrevocably from the boom period of industrialised mining, the special historic character of Alston Moor presents a number of contemporary conservation challenges that will remain in place for the foreseeable future. The economy of the area is increasingly dominated by service industries often related to tourism and the continuance of a small manufacturing base, but improved communication technologies will continue to have a significant effect on the kind of jobs and businesses that the

Figure 111
Ruined farmstead in the Nent Valley near Whitehall.
[DP154133]

129

area can sustain. Since 2001, an initiative called Cybermoor – funded by Defra and the European Union – has established the infrastructure for high-speed broadband communication across the parish by means of satellite and fibre-optic technology, and developed a community web portal that supports local businesses and provides a range of useful communication tools for the community as a whole. As home-working and e-commerce businesses are made more viable by enhanced internet access, there is the potential for rising demand in the property market and the area's historic assets may prove particularly attractive. Work led by English Heritage in other parts of England has revealed how farmsteads are emerging as hubs of up-and-coming digital economies, being more strongly associated with home-based entrepreneurial businesses than any other kind of urban or rural property.[63]

As the economy and population of the area continue to evolve, however, new ways in which these challenges can be tackled will emerge and have already begun to do so. There is some limited scope for further formal protection of heritage assets in the area through inclusion on the National Heritage List for England, but there are a range of everyday issues in the conservation of the area's heritage that cannot be solved by such an approach, however worthwhile it may be for the small number of individual structures affected. There are a number of factors that exist outside the local planning system that have the potential to influence positively the ways in which historic buildings can be cared for and sensitively enhanced. For instance, Natural England administers grants to farmers offered through Environmental Stewardship for the maintenance of farm buildings, which is a popular option in upland areas of England, and also for the conservation repair of a much smaller selection of buildings.

Beyond these individual efforts, there are a set of broader social and economic trends that suggest numerous developing opportunities to enhance protection for the area's heritage. The growth of tourism, linked strongly to the landscape and history of the area, is likely to continue, and this will increase demand for numerous different services – for example, exhibition space, overnight accommodation of various shapes and sizes, and hospitality venues – the vast majority of which are likely to be housed in existing and renovated buildings. The tourism themes of pursuing landscape beauty, outdoor activities and historic interest have been supplemented with artistic facilities such as the Art

Apartments in The Butts and a number of gallery venues, and attractions like these will continue to develop alongside interest in Alston Moor's core value as a place of extraordinary industrial and natural heritage.

The use of appropriate local materials (or closely matched equivalents) is obviously a key concern for restoration projects both on farms and in the larger settlements, as is the retention of key historic features such as chimneys, fireplaces and original doorways and window openings. The use of non-traditional materials like uPVC in fittings such as doors and windows is an additional key concern, both within and especially outside the parish's two Conservation Areas, if the consistent appearance of historic buildings and streetscapes is to be maintained. Alston Moor (in common with other upland areas) will always have particular problems resisting the use of such materials as they are perceived as the means to insulate buildings more efficiently and cost-effectively against an often harsh climate, though it is worth noting that recent research has demonstrated the high performance that can be achieved with traditional windows without sacrificing their historic character.

In particular, and with reference to the Local Plan devised by Eden Council, there is a pool of derelict and semi-derelict buildings that scatter the landscape, typically but not exclusively related to farming or mining, and these must be found new uses if they are to survive as visible components of the historic environment. The area has a very high level of survival of traditional farmsteads, with 84 per cent of farmsteads retaining much of their *c* 1900 form. This is largely, although not wholly, due to the high proportion of linear farmsteads which tend to retain the attached working buildings even after the farm's working practices, or the building uses, have changed. This level of survival in the Alston area is slightly higher than across the North Pennines generally, where 80 per cent of farmsteads retain their historic character, and is similar to that of other upland areas of England where farmsteads have been mapped and the level of 20th-century change recorded.

Bastles and houses-over-byres pose considerable questions for the future. It has not been necessary to live on the first floor for reasons of security for several centuries, while advances in insulation and in heating have rendered the rising heat from animals confined on the ground floor unnecessary for domestic comfort. Many have been used for years for agricultural storage, and developments in farming equipment have sometimes resulted in alterations such as

Figure 112
The 1735 portion of Annat Walls was refloored, refenestrated and replanned in the 1980s; the external staircase was also removed. The adjacent bastle range in the foreground of the photograph has, however, been recently consolidated in a much more sympathetic manner. [DP109787]

the removal of internal floors and the enlarging of doorways. In certain instances where bastles have been brought back into domestic use, altering the arrangement of floor levels to create a more typical plan, the underlying rationale of local practices and the story they tell has been radically compromised (Fig 112). Many farmsteads face the long-term abandonment of older buildings altogether, as today farmers require large, modern, lightweight structures with greater flexibility of use. This is a widespread issue across the uplands of northern England. For hard-pressed farmers there is little reason to maintain or repair traditional buildings unless they have a use, and gradual dereliction can result. However, not only do bastle-type buildings have general appeal, but they are particularly suitable – in both town and country – for a modern 'live-work' environment, with the separation of functions already expressed in their historic form and offering much-needed storage. There have been numerous examples of formerly ruined bastles and bastle-related vernacular buildings that have been upgraded to modern living standards, such as Bunkershill,

Figure 113
Bunkershill restored.
[DP154135]

Lambrigg and Middle Bayles (Fig 113). Though these buildings are not prominent landmarks on major roads and are not typically seen by many people, their restoration does much to repair and enhance the fine grain of historic interest and quality across Alston Moor as a whole.

The re-use of industrial buildings continues to be a challenge nationwide (Fig 114). High Mill, one of Alston's most important industrial structures, located in the centre of the town's conservation area and complete with its important overshot waterwheel, is now largely disused and may become subject to redevelopment pressures. Nenthead, whose raison d'être dwindled with the end of the lead industry, has little formal protection, and the character of Hillersdon Terrace has long since been changed by the addition of extensions, conservatories, porches and enlarged windows. The national decline in religious observance in most Christian denominations has led to a particular threat to Nonconformist chapels, including the important and elegant former Congregational chapel at Redwing. The redundancy of all of Alston Moor's purpose-built Methodist chapels poses a considerable challenge, the chapels standing empty whilst decisions are made about their future use and development.

English Heritage has a key role to play in managing this process of change in the historic environment. This book is the result of one aspect of that role, identifying what is important about a particular locality, its development and the features which attest to it. Ultimately, management of the historic environment of Alston Moor depends on input and collaboration from a range of bodies, including Eden District Council (as planning authority), the North Pennines AONB Partnership, Defra, the Environment Agency and Natural England, as well as the owners and occupiers of the buildings and landscape that make up this very special place.

Figure 114
The remains of lead mines above Nenthead, with the mid 19th-century Assay House.
[DP154353]

Notes

Abbreviations:

CAS – Cumbria Archive Service, Carlisle

DUL – Durham University Library, Durham

NEIMME – North of England Institute of Mining and Mechanical Engineers, Newcastle

TNA – The National Archives, London

1   Denton 2003, 344.

2   Hunt 1970, 187; Wallace 1890, 11.

3   Sopwith 1833, 17–18.

4   Jollie 1811, part II, 52.

5   Camden 1607, 649.

6   Robertson 1998, 9.

7   Wallace 1890, 9.

8   Sharp 1908, 280.

9   Wallace 1890, 11.

10 Ibid, 6–7.

11 Winchester 2000, 160–5.

12 DUL DPR Reg. VI, ff. 113v–14: will of Christopher Walton, Alston, 1 Nov 1585.

13 DUL DPRI/1/1672/W5/1.

14 Winchester 2000, 160, citing R. S. Ferguson (ed), *A Cursory Relation of all the Antiquities and Familyes in Cumberland by Edmond Sandford, circa 1675*, Cumberland and Westmorland Antiquarian and Archaeological Society Tract Series, IV, 1890, 47 and CAS D/Lons/Thomas Denton MS, 122.

15 Wood 1798, 292–3.

16 *Gentleman's Magazine* 1747, 385.

17 Robertson 1998, 10.

18 Sopwith 1833, 19, 21.

19 Brewer 1867, 1312.

20 Bain 1896, 80.

21 Lambeth Palace Library, Shrewsbury Papers MS696/Folio 7: Sir Thomas Hylton to the Earl of Shrewsbury, and the Council of the North, from Tynemouth, Northumberland, 30 November 1555.

22 Denton 2003, 343.

23 Sopwith 1833, 24.

24 Mackenzie 1827, 532, 539; *Gentleman's Magazine* 1821, 234–5.

25 Firth and Rait 1911, 623–52: 'November 1652: An Additional Act for Sale of several Lands and Estates forfeited to the Commonwealth for Treason.'

26 CAS Q/11/1/8/20: Petition, undated but 1688, of Thomas Vipond of Alston – bay mare stolen from the Upper Crag, Garrigill, in Alston Moor; CAS Q/11/1/18/7: Petition, undated but 1691, of the parishioners of Alston Moor, asking for the better securing of the County from theft, as of old, as they have lost 8 valuable horses since 14th May; CAS Q/11/1/65/21: Petition, undated but 1702, of Joseph Walton of Alston Moor – gelding stolen, worth £3.10; CAS Q/11/1/73/22: Petition, undated but 1704, of Thomas Lee of Alston – bay mare stolen, worth £3 or upwards.

27 Wallace 1890, 17.

28 TNA 75/188: 15 August 1697, deed signed by the Hon. Francis Radcliffe in the name of the earl of Derwentwater to Thomas Errington of Corby Gates, gent., allowing him to build a shop in Alston on the common there; 23 October 1703, as above, to Joseph Clocker of Alston.

29 Hunt 1970, 2.

30 Thain 1999, 25.

31 Williams 1975, 93.

32 Raistrick 1988, 88.

33 CAS CCH 3/1, Cumberland Highway Papers, 1879–84.

34 Hunt 1970, 40.

35 Ibid, 147.

36 Pennant 1801, 187.

37 Svedenstierna 1973, 166.

38 Robertson 1998, 36–7.

39 Jollie 1811, part I, 77.

40 CAS QRZ 10, maps 1 and 5.

41 Sopwith 1833, 26.

42 Wallace 1890, 47.

43 1864 Parliamentary Report by Dr Peacock, *Conditions in mines to which the provisions of the Act 23 and 24 Victoria c. 151 do not apply, with reference to the health and safety of persons employed*, quoted in Hunt 1970, 142.

44 Ibid.

45 Hunt 1970, 226.

46 White 1859, 44.

47 Figures from the 1840 minutes of Committee of Council on Education and 1851 Religious Census, quoted in Hunt 1970, 220.

48 Pennant 1801, 187.

49 Hodgson 1840, 25.

50 Ibid.

51 Robertson 1998, 71.

52 Ibid.

53 Ibid, 72.

54 Ibid, 73.

55 Thain 1999, 13–14.

56 Robertson 1998, 75.

57 Kelly's 1906, 27.

58 Ibid, 26.

59 Mackenzie 1825, II, 321.

60 TNA ADM 169/558 and 669: purchase of Ivy House, Garrigill, 1928–9 and Gatehead Farm, 1934.

61 See Edwards and Lake 2012.

62 http://www.eden.gov.uk/planning-and-development/historic-environment-conservation/conservation-areas/.

63 These methods are described in greater detail in Historic Farm Buildings: Extending the Evidence Base (2009). For the West Midlands Farmsteads and Landscapes Project see http://www.english-heritage.org.uk/wmidlandsfarmsteads.

References and further reading

Bain, J (ed) 1896 *Calendar of Border Papers, Vol 2: 1595–1603*. Edinburgh: HMSO

Brewer, J S (ed) 1867 *Letters and Papers, Foreign and Domestic, of the reign of Henry VIII, Vol 3: 1519–1523*. London: HMSO

Camden, W 1607 *Britannia, sive florentissimorum regnorum Angliae, Scotiae, Hiberniae* … London: George Bishop and John Norton; 1 edn 1586

Denton, T 2003 *A Perambulation of Cumberland 1687–1688* …, ed Winchester, A and Wane, M. Woodbridge: Boydell Press

Durham, K 2008 *Strongholds of the Border Reivers: Fortifications of the Anglo-Scottish Border 1296–1603*. Oxford: Osprey Publishing

Edwards, B and Lake J 2012 *Historic Farmsteads and Landscape Character in the North Pennines*. Wimborne: Forum Heritage Services; unpublished report for Natural England and English Heritage

Firth, C H and Rait, R 1911 *Acts and Ordinances of the Interregnum, 1642–1660*. London: HMSO

Forster, W 1883 *A Treatise on a Section of the Strata from Newcastle-upon-Tyne to Cross Fell* … Newcastle upon Tyne: Andrew Reid; 1 edn 1809

Gentleman's Magazine, ed Sylvanus Urban [Edward Cave], Vol 17, August 1747, 384–5. London: E Cave

Gentleman's Magazine, ed Sylvanus Urban [Edward Cave], Vol 91, Part 1, March 1821, 234–5. London: John Nichols & Son

Hodgson, J 1840 *History of Northumberland*, Part II, Vol III. Newcastle upon Tyne

Hunt, C J 1970 *The Lead Miners of the Northern Pennines in the Eighteenth and Nineteenth Centuries*. New York: Augustus M Kelley

Jollie, F 1811 *Jollie's Cumberland Guide & Directory* …, Parts I & II. Carlisle: F Jollie and Sons

Kelly's 1906 *Kelly's Directory of Cumberland*. London: Kelly's Directories Ltd

Kelly's 1938 *Kelly's Directory of Cumberland and Westmorland*. London: Kelly's

Mackenzie, E 1825 *An Historical, Topographical, and Descriptive View of the County of Northumberland …*, Vol II. Newcastle upon Tyne: Mackenzie and Dent

Mackenzie, E 1827 *A Descriptive and Historical Account of the Town and County of Newcastle-upon-Tyne, including the Borough of Gateshead*: Newcastle upon Tyne: Mackenzie and Dent

North Pennines Town Project Group, 1999 'Alston: Study of Buildings'. Unpublished report

Pennant, T 1801 *A Tour from Downing to Alston-Moor*. London: Oriental Press

Perriam, D R and Robinson, J 1998 *The Medieval Fortified Buildings of Cumbria*. Cumberland and Westmorland Antiquarian and Archaeological Society

Raistrick, A 1988 *Two Centuries of Industrial Welfare. The London (Quaker) Lead Company 1692–1905*. Littleborough & Newcastle upon Tyne: Kelsall & Davis

Ramm, H G, McDowall, R W and Mercer, E 1970 *Shielings and Bastles*. London: HMSO

Robertson, A 1998 *A History of Alston Moor* (2nd edn, 2010). Alston: Hundy Publications

Robertson, A 2012 *The Foreigners in the Hills: the Vieille Montagne Zinc Company of Belgium on Alston Moor*. Alston: Hundy Publications

Ryder, P 1992 'Bastles and Bastle-Like Buildings in Allendale, Northumberland'. *Archaeological Journal*, **149**, 351–379

Ryder, P 1996 *Bastle Houses in the Northern Pennines*. Nenthead: North Pennines Heritage Trust

Sharp, J 1908 *Calendar of Inquisitions Post Mortem and other Analogous Documents Preserved in the Public Record Office*, Vol V, Edward II. London: HMSO

Sopwith, T 1833 *An Account of the Mining Districts of Alston Moor, Weardale, and Teesdale, in Cumberland and Durham ...* Alnwick: W. Davison

Svedenstierna, E 1973, *Svedenstierna's Tour of Great Britain 1802–3: The Travel Diary of an Industrial Spy*, trans. Dellow, E L. Newton Abbot: David & Charles

Thain, L 1999 *Through the Ages: The Story of Nenthead*. Nenthead: Women's Institute and North Pennines Heritage Trust

Wallace, W 1890 *Alston Moor: Its Pastoral People: Its Mines And Miners; from the Earliest Periods to Recent Times*. Newcastle: Mawson, Swan & Morgan

White, W 1859 *Northumberland and the Border*. London: Chapman and Hall

Wilkinson, P 2009 *Old Alston*. Catrine: Stenlake Publishing

Williams, L A 1975 *Road Transport in Cumbria in the 19th century*. London: George Allen and Unwin

Winchester, A 2000 *The Harvest of the Hills: Rural Life in Northern England and the Scottish Borders, 1400–1700*. Edinburgh: Edinburgh University Press

Wood, H (ed) 1798 *A Collection of Decrees by the Court of Exchequer in tithe-causes, from the Usurpation to the present time* [1650–1798], Vol II. London: Bunney, Thompson, and Co.

Other titles in the Informed Conservation series

Berwick-upon-Tweed: Three places, two nations, one town.
Adam Menuge with Catherine Dewar, 2009.
Product code 51471, ISBN 9781848020290

Bridport and West Bay: The buildings of the flax and hemp industry.
Mike Williams, 2006.
Product code 51167, ISBN 9781873592861

Defending Scilly.
Mark Bowden and Allan Brodie, 2011.
Product code 51530, ISBN 9781848020436

England's Schools: History, architecture and adaptation.
Elain Harwood, 2010.
Product code 51476, ISBN 9781848020313

Gateshead: Architecture in a changing English urban landscape.
Simon Taylor and David Lovie, 2004.
Product code 52000, ISBN 9781873592762

Manchester: The warehouse legacy – An introduction and guide.
Simon Taylor, Malcolm Cooper and P S Barnwell, 2002.
Product code 50668, ISBN 9781873592670

Newcastle's Grainger Town: An urban renaissance.
Fiona Cullen and David Lovie, 2003.
Product code 50811, ISBN 9781873592779

'One Great Workshop': The buildings of the Sheffield metal trades.
Nicola Wray, Bob Hawkins and Colum Giles, 2001.
Product code 50214, ISBN 9781873592663

Plymouth: Vision of a modern city.
Jeremy Gould, 2010.
Product code 51531, ISBN 9781848020504

Stourport-on-Severn: Pioneer town of the canal age.
Colum Giles, Keith Falconer, Barry Jones and Michael Taylor, 2007.
Product code 51290, ISBN 9781905624362

Further information on titles in the Informed Conservation series can be found on our website.
To order through EH Sales
Tel: 01235 465577
Fax: 01235 465556
Email: direct.order@marston.co.uk
Online bookshop: www.english-heritageshop.org.uk

Alston town map.
[© Crown Copyright and database right 2013. All rights reserved. Ordnance Survey Licence number 100024900]

Back cover
The entrance into Haggs Mine, Alston Moor.
[DP143584]